HOL

TRIVIA

OVER 300 CURIOUS
LISTS FROM TINSELTOWN

HOLLYWOOD TRIVIA

OVER 300 CURIOUS
LISTS FROM TINSELTOWN

Aubrey Malone

First published in Great Britain in 1999
This paperback edition published in 2004 by

Prion
an imprint of the
Carlton Publishing Group
20 Mortimer Street
London W1T 3JW

ISBN 1-85375-499-4

A catalogue record for this book is available from the
British Library

Printed in Great Britain
by Mackays

Subjects A-Z

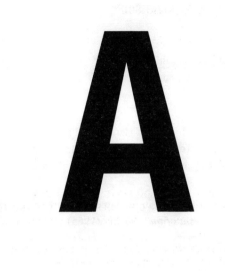

BREAK A LEG!
10 accidents on movie sets

JAY C. FLIPPEN
Developed an infection in his leg while shooting *Cat Ballou* (1965), which turned gangrenous, resulting in its eventual amputation.

GAYLORD LLOYD
This unit director (a brother of Harold) had his eye knocked out by copper splinters from exploding dynamite caps during the garage massacre scene from Howard Hawks' *Scarface* (1932).

PAUL MANTZ
This stunt pilot who stood in for James Stewart during the making of *The Flight of the Phoenix* (1965) was killed when the single-engine plane he was flying crashed as he was trying to land it.

DUSTIN HOFFMAN
Shot himself during a scene in *Little Big Man* (1970) when he tried to draw his gun from a holster too fast using real bullets.

AUDREY HEPBURN
Broke her back during a horse-riding scene in John Huston's *The Unforgiven* (1959).

JIM CARREY
Came out second best in a screen brawl with wrestler Jerry Lawler while making *Man in the Moon* (1999). Lawler was just a bit too authentic, sending old rubber-face to the hospital in a neck brace.

FRED ASTAIRE
Broke no fewer than a dozen canes during a dance scene in *Top Hat* (1935).

KARL MALDEN
Dislocated Marlon Brando's shoulder when pushing him during the shower scene in *A Streetcar Named Desire* (1951).

RITA HAYWORTH
Knocked out two of Glenn Ford's teeth during their fight in *Gilda* (1946).

JOHN GARFIELD
Knocked himself out when he hit a camera boom during one of the fight scenes from *Body and Soul* (1947).

STARDOOM
10 celebrities who died in accidents

VIC MORROW
Decapitated by the rotor blade of a helicopter when filming *Twilight Zone: The Movie* (1981) after a special-effects explosion went horribly wrong.

JAYNE MANSFIELD
Also decapitated, in a horrific car crash when she was only 34.

JEFFREY HUNTER
Died after a fall in his house at the age of 44.

JAMES DEAN
Broke his neck in September 1955 in a horrific car crash days after the filming of *Giant* ended. (The director had prohibited him from driving until then, being only too aware of his penchant for speed.)

CAROLE LOMBARD
Killed in a plane crash at the age of 34, leaving a devastated Clark Gable behind.

GRACE KELLY
Plunged 120 feet to her death in 1982 after her brakes failed. Ironically, the accident happened in the place where Kelly had shot a scene from *To Catch a Thief* (1955) 27 years before.

LESLIE HOWARD
Shot down by German fighters in 1943 on a flight where he was rumored to be a decoy for Winston Churchill.

NATALIE WOOD
Victim of a mysterious drowning in November 1981 after an apparent argument between Robert Wagner and Christopher Walken, costar of her last movie, *Brainstorm*, released two years later.

ALAN J. PAKULA
This acclaimed director died in November 1998, when he lost control of his car after a metal pipe flew into his windscreen. He was pronounced dead an hour later.

BUTTERFLY MCQUEEN
Winner of an Oscar in 1939 for her part in *Gone with the Wind*, she was burned to death trying to light a lantern in 1995.

AN ACTOR'S LIFE FOR ME
10 actors on acting

ROBIN WILLIAMS
Likens the experience of "corpsing" (laughing involuntarily while acting on stage) to being "circumcised in the Grand Canyon."

MEL GIBSON
Said he was goofing around all his life anyway, so he thought he might as well get paid for it.

MICKEY ROURKE
Claims he would prefer the word "animal" on his passport to "actor."

CLIFF ROBERTSON
Compares it to "standing up in a canoe with your pants down."

DAVID NIVEN
It's "being wonderfully overpaid for dressing up and playing games."

KIRK DOUGLAS
"If you write a book, you ask: 'Do you like my book?' If you paint a picture, you say: 'Do you like the picture I painted?' But if you become an actor you say: 'Do you like me?' That's why it's so painful if people say they don't."

JEREMY IRONS
Says acting is like making love: better if your partner is good, but still possible if she isn't.

KENNETH WILLIAMS
Believed there were only two maxims to be observed to make a go of it: always watch your fly, and blow your nose before you come out.

MARLON BRANDO
His passport lists him as shepherd rather than actor.

WILFRED HYDE-WHITE
Once said he learned two things at R.A.D.A.: first that he couldn't act...and second, that it didn't matter.

IT HAPPENED ONE NIGHT
40 affairs that began on film sets

Humphrey Bogart and Lauren Bacall (*To Have and Have Not*, 1945)
Barbra Streisand and Omar Sharif (*Funny Girl*, 1968)
William Hurt and Marlee Matlin (*Children of a Lesser God*, 1986)
John Malkovich and Michelle Pfeiffer (*Dangerous Liaisons*, 1988)
Warren Beatty and Madonna (*Dick Tracy*, 1990)
Julia Roberts and Kiefer Sutherland (*Flatliners*, 1990)
Brad Pitt and Gwyneth Paltrow (*Seven*, 1995)
Burt Reynolds and Sally Field (*Smokey and the Bandit*, 1977)
Steve McQueen and Ali MacGraw (*The Getaway*, 1972)
Jeff Goldblum and Laura Dern (*Jurassic Park*, 1993)
Gabriel Byrne and Ellen Barkin (*Siesta*, 1987)
Mickey Rourke and Carrie Otis (*Wild Orchid*, 1990)
Ryan O'Neal and Ali MacGraw (*Love Story*, 1970)
Susan Sarandon and Tim Robbins (*Bull Durham*, 1988)
Tom Cruise and Nicole Kidman (*Far and Away*, 1992)
Julia Roberts and Lyle Lovett (*The Player*, 1992)
Warren Beatty and Annette Bening (*Bugsy*, 1991)
Jessica Lange and Sam Shepard (*Frances*, 1982)
Madonna and Sean Penn (*Shanghai Surprise*, 1986)
Clint Eastwood and Jean Seberg (*Paint Your Wagon*, 1969)
Nastassja Kinski and Roman Polanski (*Tess*, 1980)
Sandra Bullock and Matthew McConaughey (*A Time to Kill*, 1996)
Clark Gable and Loretta Young (*The Call of the Wild*, 1935)
Marlon Brando and Pina Pellicer (*One-Eyed Jacks*, 1961)
Peter Bogdanovich and Cybill Shepherd (*The Last Picture Show*, 1971)
Jane Fonda and Donald Sutherland (*Klute*, 1971)
Spencer Tracy and Loretta Young (*A Man's Castle*, 1933)
Eleanor Parker and Robert Taylor (*Above and Beyond*, 1952)

Elvis Presley and Ann Margret (*Viva Las Vegas*, 1964)

Yves Montand and Marilyn Monroe (*Let's Make Love*, 1960)

Marlene Dietrich and Gary Cooper (*Morocco*, 1930)

Bette Davis and Gary Merrill (*All About Eve*, 1950)

Vanessa Redgrave and Franco Nero (*Camelot*, 1967)

Claire Bloom and Sydney Chaplin (*Limelight*, 1952)

Charles Bronson and Jill Ireland (*The Great Escape*, 1963)

Rita Hayworth and Glenn Ford (*Gilda*, 1946)

Grace Kelly and Ray Milland (*Dial M for Murder*, 1954)

Warren Beatty and Diane Keaton (*Reds*, 1981)

Mary Steenburgen and Malcolm MacDowell (*Time After Time*, 1979)

Matthew Broderick and Jennifer Grey (*Ferris Bueller's Day Off*, 1986)

AFFAIRS TO REMEMBER
20 couples that came close to marriage

Clara Bow and Gary Cooper

Ryan O' Neal and Farrah Fawcett

Kiefer Sutherland and Julia Roberts

Brad Pitt and Gwyneth Paltrow

Gary Cooper and Patricia Neal

Elvis Presley and Ann Margret

Warren Beatty and Joan Collins

Joan Crawford and Clark Gable

Spencer Tracy and Katharine Hepburn

Rex Harrison and Lilli Palmer

Howard Hughes and Carole Lombard

Marilyn Monroe and Yves Montand

Tyrone Power and Lana Turner
Johnny Depp and Winona Ryder
Roger Vadim and Catherine Deneuve
Victor Mature and Rita Hayworth
Frank Sinatra and Lauren Bacall
Natalie Wood and James Dean
Tom Cruise and Rebecca de Mornay
Burt Reynolds and Sally Field

ACT YOUR AGE

10 on-screen age discrepancies

Angela Lansbury played Laurence Harvey's mother in *The Manchurian Candidate* (1962), but she was only three years older than him at the time.

Barbara Bel Geddes, who played Larry Hagman's mother in the hit TV series *Dallas*, was only nine years older than him.

Rod Steiger is a year younger than Marlon Brando, yet he played his older brother in *On the Waterfront* (1954).

Rosemary de Camp played James Cagney's mother in *Yankee Doodle Dandy* (1942), but in real life she was fourteen years younger than him.

Sean Connery played Harrison Ford's father in *Indiana Jones and the Last Crusade* (1989), even though he's only twelve years older than him.

In *The Graduate* (1967) Katharine Ross plays Anne Bancroft's daughter; there are only eleven years between them in real life.

Cary Grant was only a year younger than his screen mother in Alfred Hitchcock's *North by Northwest* (1959).

Richard Ney played Greer Garson's son in *Mrs. Miniver* (1942). A couple of years later they married one another.

In *The Entertainer* (1960), Joan Plowright played Laurence Olivier's daughter, but in real life they were husband and wife.

Sissy Spacek played country singer Loretta Lynn as a 13-year-old for the early scenes of *Coalminer's Daughter* (1982) while she herself was 31.

LOCK UP YOUR DAUGHTERS
10 age gaps between leading men and women

Entrapment (1998)
Sean Connery thirty-nine years older than Catherine Zeta Jones.

A Perfect Murder (1998)
Michael Douglas twenty-eight years older than his screen wife Gwyneth Paltrow.

Six Days, Seven Nights (1998)
Harrison Ford twenty-seven years older than Anne Heche.

As Good As It Gets (1998)
Jack Nicholson twenty-six years older than Helen Hunt.

The Horse Whisperer (1998)
Robert Redford twenty-three years older than Kristin Scott
Thomas.

Mad Dog and Glory (1993)
Robert de Niro twenty-seven years older than Uma Thurman.

Absence of Malice (1981)
Paul Newman twenty-one years older than Sally Field.

The Fountainhead (1949)
Gary Cooper twenty-six years older than Patricia Neal
(they fell for one another off-screen as well).

Charade (1963)
Cary Grant twenty-five years older than Audrey Hepburn.

Rio Bravo (1959)
John Wayne twenty-four years older than Angie Dickinson.

5 REAL-LIFE AGE DISCREPANCIES

LAUREN BACALL
Born in 1924, the same year her future husband Humphrey
Bogart got married for the first time.

MIA FARROW
Her mother was only four years older than her former husband
Frank Sinatra.

WARREN BEATTY
When he was nominated for an Oscar for *Splendor in the Grass*
(1961), his present wife Annette Bening was just 3 years old.

GINA LOLLOBRIGIDA
When she appeared with Tony Curtis in *Trapeze* (1956), he
was 30 and she was 33. However, says Curtis, "Five years

later she was 31. When I reached 40 I read somewhere that she was 27."

ZSA ZSA GABOR
Once produced a birth certificate for curious journalists specifying that she was at that time 54 years of age. If this were true, however, as Sheilah Graham observed, she would only have been 13 years of age when she got married for the first time.

BARFLIES
5 comic alcoholics

DUDLEY MOORE, *Arthur* (1981)
Erupts into manic laughter every time he's had one over the eight —or even one over the one. Maybe the fact that he's rich helps.

MICHAEL CAINE, *Educating Rita* (1983)
This cockney version of Dylan Thomas makes a practice of falling off college lecterns, like all good boozy profs. Of course, that all changes when he becomes a Svengali of sorts to Julie Walters, who weans him off hard liquor.

ERROL FLYNN, *The Sun Also Rises* (1957)
Flynn has a lot of fun bitching about how awful life is in fairly typical Hemingwayese as he runs with the bulls in Pamplona… spouting a lot of bull himself in the process.

LEE MARVIN, *Cat Ballou* (1965)
Marvin likes getting soused so much he even gets his hoss tipsy.

GENE WILDER, *Blazing Saddles* (1974)
Wilder is an alcoholic cowpoke who suffers from a shaky trigger finger. Oh, and some flatulence.

ON THE ROCKS
and 5 tragic alcoholics

JACK LEMMON, *Days of Wine and Roses* (1962)
Starts off happy, but soon reduced to animal level as he frantic-
ally searches for a stash of booze in pop-in-law's greenhouse.
Wife Lee Remick follows suit, with even more tragic results.

RAY MILLAND, *The Lost Weekend* (1945)
Milland is a frustrated writer who hides The Hard Stuff every-
where you ever thought of (including the trusty old lampshade)
before finally succumbing to the ultimate nadir for a writer:
hocking his typewriter for another refill.

MEG RYAN, *When a Man Loves a Woman* (1994)
Ryan finds herself reduced to riffling through the garbage for
dregs of vodka bottles, but then she goes into rehab and gets her
life back, which means shifting of goal posts in her relationship
with patient hubby Andy Garcia.

NICOLAS CAGE, *Leaving Las Vegas* (1995)
Hopeless alcoholic Nic Cage decides to drink himself to that big
battleship in the sky and there ain't a darn thing tart-with-a-heart
Elisabeth Shue can do about it, 'cept to ease him on his way to
Boot Hill with some tender loving care—and a few hip flasks of
rocket gas.

PIPER LAURIE, *The Hustler* (1961)
"I'm not drunk," she says to pool shark Paul Newman as she
stumbles coming out of a pub, "I'm a cripple." But it's not long
before the pair of them are slurping it up bigtime, and she's
eventually tipped over the edge by unscrupulous agent George
C. Scott after Newman deserts her for the green baize.

STARS AND BARS
5 real-life guzzlers

MICHAEL CAINE
Claimed the best research for playing a drunk was being a British actor for twenty years.

PETER O'TOOLE
When he and Peter Finch were refused an after-hours drink in an Irish pub one night, they found a way around the problem by buying the pub!

ERROL FLYNN
Used to bring oranges on to film sets and squirt them full of vodka with a hypodermic syringe.

RICHARD BURTON
One of the few times in his life this hopeless alcoholic remained sober was when he was called on to play drunks, "because I didn't know how to play them when I was drunk."

W. C. FIELDS
Always kept a flask of martini on set with him, pretending it was pineapple juice. One day somebody called his bluff, causing him to come out with the immortal line, "Somebody's put pineapple juice in my pineapple juice."

THE LAND THAT TIME FORGOT
10 movie anachronisms

The Wrong Box (1966)
Set in Victorian times, but you can see TV antennas on the roofs of some of the houses.

Stagecoach (1939)
Tire tracks are visible in the desert sand during this western set in the late nineteenth century.

The Last Temptation of Christ (1988)
Jesus wears a robe with double-seamed machine stitches: a pretty natty sartorial trick for the Holy Land in 30 A.D.

The Story of Robin Hood and His Merrie Men (1952)
Maid Marian wears a dress with a zipper in one scene.

A Tale of Two Cities (1958)
A newspaper here shows a dispatch from Reuters, but Reuters' inventor wasn't even born at the time the film is set.

Gone with the Wind (1939)
An electric streetlamp is visible in one of the scenes.

El Cid (1961)
One of the extras in this eleventh-century adventure story can be seen wearing sunglasses.

Camelot (1967)
King Arthur can be seen wearing a Band-aid on his neck at
one stage.

The Crusades (1935)
In this Cecil B. De Mille offering, set in medieval times, a king
flips his cape back to reveal…a watch.

Shane (1953)
As the buckskin-clad hero rides into the valley in the opening
scene, you can clearly see the dust raised by a passing car.

DECONSTRUCTING HARRY
10 actor anagrams

CLINT EASTWOOD
Old West action

MARLON BRANDO
Alarm! Don born

WOODY ALLEN
A lewd loony

WARREN BEATTY
Watery banter

SEAN CONNERY
On any screen

TOM CRUISE
I'm so cuter

LEONARDO DiCAPRIO
Adored in cool pair

MICHAEL DOUGLAS
Eh! I am a cold slug

MEL GIBSON
Limbs 'n' ego

DUSTIN HOFFMAN
Offhand, I'm nuts

10 ACTRESS ANAGRAMS

JENNIFER ANISTON
Fine in torn jeans

BARBRA STREISAND
I bear star's brand

JULIA ROBERTS
I lure star job

BETTE DAVIS
Best TV idea

DEMI MOORE
Moodier Me

GRETA GARBO
Go grab tear

MAE WEST
Am sweet

KATE WINSLET
Wet skin tale

MARLENE DIETRICH
The mild are nicer

SOPHIA LOREN
O, no real hips

WHAT DID YOU DO IN THE WAR DADDY?

10 stars whose ancestors fought in the American Civil War

Carole Lombard (Ralph Cheney)
Steve McQueen (Thomas McQueen)
Lee Marvin (Major General Henry Lee)
Raymond Massey (Jonathan Massey)
John Wayne (Isaac Buck)
Bing Crosby (Enoch Crosby)
John Lithgow (Major William Lithgow)

Ginger Rogers (James McGrath)
Shirley Temple (William Amberson)
Robert Taylor (George Michael Spangler)

HEAVENLY BODIES
15 stars who've played angels

Jessica Lange (*All That Jazz*, 1980)
Holly Hunter (*A Life Less Ordinary*, 1997)
Henry Travers (*It's A Wonderful Life*, 1946)
John Philip Law (*Barbarella*, 1968)
Diane Cilento (*The Angel Who Pawned Her Harp*, 1954)
James Mason (*Forever Darling*, 1956)
Cary Grant (*The Bishop's Wife*, 1947)
Robert Cummings (*Heaven Only Knows*, 1947)
Edmund Gwenn (*For Heaven's Sake*, 1950)
Jack Benny (*The Horn Blows at Midnight*, 1945)
Claude Rains (*Here Comes Mr. Jordan*, 1941)
Jeanette MacDonald (*I Married an Angel*, 1942)
Harry Dean Stanton (*One Magic Christmas*, 1985)
John Travolta (*Michael*, 1996)
Debra Winger (*Made in Heaven*, 1987)

ANIMAL CRACKERS
stars, pets, and animals

ROY ROGERS
Was so devoted to his horse Trigger that when it died he had it
stuffed and mounted.

JOHN BARRYMORE
Had a pet vulture named Maloney. He fed it on rotten meat,
obtained by scavenging in his neighbors' garbage cans early in
the morning.

SHIRLEY TEMPLE
To get her to cry in films, unscrupulous directors would tell her
that her pets were dead.

RIN TIN TIN
Was the only dog in the world to have had his own dressing
room, chauffeur-driven limousine, and personal valet.

ROSEANNE
She once put a rabbit into a washing machine because its feet
were dirty.

RONALD REAGAN
His chimpanzee costar in *Bedtime for Bonzo* (1951) died the day
before the film's première. (Did he know something that the
makers didn't?)

CLINT EASTWOOD
Once said the high point of his career wasn't donning a Magnum
or a spaghetti western poncho, but appearing opposite an orang-
utan in *Every Which Way But Loose* (1978).

LORNE GREENE
Had one of his nipples bitten off by an alligator while filming
Wild Kingdom (1989).

MICHAEL ANDERSON
This director put 8,552 animals in all into *Around the World in Eighty Days* (1956).

AVA GARDNER
When she died, she left her dog Morgan his own maid and limo, plus a monthly allowance.

THE EYE OF THE BEHOLDER
10 stars on their appearance

PHYLLIS DILLER
"My photographs don't do me justice: they look just like me."

ROBERT MITCHUM
"People think I have an interesting walk. Hell, I'm just trying to keep my gut in."

CHARLES BRONSON
"I look like a quarry someone has dynamited."

SPENCER TRACY
"This mug of mine is as plain as a barn door. Why should people pay thirty-five cents to see it?"

MARLON BRANDO
"I have eyes like a dead pig."

CHARLES LAUGHTON
"I have a face like the behind of an elephant."

DAVID NIVEN
"I look like a cross between two pounds of halibut and an explosion in an old clothes closet."

FRANKIE HOWERD
"Descriptions of my face have included comparisons with most root vegetables."

SYLVESTER STALLONE
"I built my body to carry my brain around in."

GWYNETH PALTROW
"Beauty to me is about being comfortable in your own skin: either that, or a kick-ass red lipstick."

THE WILD BUNCH
10 celebs who were arrested

RICHARD DREYFUSS
In 1979 after crashing his car under the influence of cocaine. "I was doing two grams of cocaine a day," he said afterwards, "as well as 20 Percodan pills and about two quarts of alcohol. The only difference between John Belushi and me is that he's dead and I'm not."

JANE FONDA
Accused of assault and battery on an airport official in 1970 when she was detained for questioning following her anti-American protests.

BRIGITTE BARDOT
For castrating a libidinous donkey that was bothering her pets.

HUGH GRANT
For lewd conduct when hooker Divine Brown was alleged to have given him oral sex on Sunset Boulevard in 1995.

MONTGOMERY CLIFT
At the beginning of his career, for consorting with a male prostitute.

QUENTIN TARANTINO
At the age of 15 for stealing an Elmore Leonard book. He has since recompensed Leonard the $3 from one of their multi-million dollar collaborations.

WOODY HARRELSON
For climbing the Golden Gate Bridge to protest at the pollution levels of the local water company.

ROBERT DOWNEY JR
By the L.A.P.D. in June 1996, for possession of heroin, cocaine, and a .357 Magnum. He was subsequently put behind bars for failing to appear at a drug-alcohol test.

MICKEY ROURKE
In July 1994, for slapping and kicking his wife Carrie Otis.

NICK NOLTE
For selling phony draft cards to teenagers. He was sentenced to 45 years in prison and given a $75,000 fine. The sentence was suspended but he is still technically a felon, so he can't vote.

PERSONAL BEST
10 athletic stars

RYAN O' NEAL
In 1970 he won the L.A. Silver Annual Handball Tournament.

BUSTER CRABBE
Won the 400-meters freestyle gold medal for swimming when he represented America at the 1932 Olympic Games.

ALAN LADD
American diving champion in 1932.

PETER SELLERS
Was vice-president of the London Judo Society for a time.

DARRYL F. ZANUCK
Is in the American Croquet Hall of Fame.

KATHARINE HEPBURN
Won a figure-skating bronze medal at Madison Square Gardens
in New York at the age of 14.

PAUL NEWMAN
Has been a professional racing driver since he appeared in the
movie *Winning* (1969).

JOHN WAYNE
Played football for the University of Southern California.

JOHNNY WEISSMULLER
Won seven Olympic gold medals in all. Clive James quipped,
"He's won so many golds, he could stay fit just carrying them
around."

JIM BROWN
This sometime professional footballer was voted Athlete of the
Year in 1964.

DON'T CALL US
10 stars' unique audition experiences

MIA FARROW
Was rejected in an audition to play one of the von Trapp children
in *The Sound of Music* (1965).

MEL GIBSON
Got the part of *Mad Max* (1979) because he'd been beaten up a

few days before the audition and his roughed-up appearance was just what the director George Miller was looking for.

Dustin Hoffman
Shortly after he completed his audition for *The Graduate* (1966), Mel Brooks told him charmingly, "You're not going to get it because you're an ugly little rat."

Sylvester Stallone
He failed his first audition because the director (Sal Mineo) said he wasn't intimidating enough for the role he was testing for. His reaction? He started intimidating Mineo!

Clint Eastwood
In his early days he was told his speech was too soft, he was too tall, he squinted too much, and his teeth needed capping. "That's all still true today," he says, "but the attitude is a little different now."

Sophia Loren
Was told her hips were too big, her nose was too long, and her mouth too big when she attended her first screen test. But she refused to take anybody's advice and stayed as she was.

Clark Gable
Failed his first screen test at Warner Brothers because Darryl F. Zanuck thought his ears were too large.

Fred Astaire
The report on an early audition said, "Can't sing, can't act. Dances a little."

Cary Grant
A casting director once informed him that he was bowlegged and that his neck was too thick.

Judy Garland
America's most famous child star of her day once failed an audition for the TV show *Our Gang*.

A LIFE LESS ORDINARY
20 classic film-star autobiographies

Ronald Reagan, *Where's the Rest of Me?*
David Niven, *The Moon's a Balloon*
Oliver Reed, *Reed All About Me*
Michael Caine, *What's it All About?*
Burt Reynolds, *My Life*
Kirk Douglas, *The Ragman's Son*
Peter O'Toole, *Loitering with Intent*
Bing Crosby, *Call Me Lucky*
Marlon Brando, *Songs My Mother Taught Me*
Peter Ustinov, *Dear Me*
Edward G. Robinson, *All My Yesterdays*
Laurence Olivier, *Confessions of an Actor*
Alec Guinness, *Blessings in Disguise*
Ali MacGraw, *Moving Pictures*
Sarah Miles, *A Right Royal Bastard*
Robert Evans, *The Kid Stays in the Picture*
Joan Crawford, *A Portrait of Joan*
Maurice Chevalier, *I Remember it Well*
Joan Collins, *Second Act*
Drew Barrymore, *Little Girl Lost*

SIGNING YOUR LIFE AWAY
5 tales of autograph hounds

SHIRLEY TEMPLE
Said she stopped believing in Santa Claus when she went to see him in a department store at the age of 12…and he asked her for her autograph.

JOAN COLLINS
Stopped giving them when she was in the bathroom one day and a piece of paper was shoved under the door, with a pen attached.

ROBERT MITCHUM
Whenever people asked him for one he used to sign it "Kirk Douglas."

ERROL FLYNN
Hit a policeman once when he asked him for his autograph in what Flynn thought a threatening manner.

DREW BARRYMORE
After she was arrested for a cocaine offense at the age of 14, the arresting officers removed her handcuffs, and then asked her for her autograph.

B

YOU'VE BEEN 'WARREN'ED
25 stars Warren Beatty was involved with

Brigitte Bardot, Annette Bening, Candice Bergen, Cher, Julie
Christie, Joan Collins, Catherine Deneuve, Faye Dunaway, Britt
Ekland, Jane Fonda, Goldie Hawn, Kate Jackson, Diane Keaton,
Vivien Leigh, Madonna, Joni Mitchell, Jackie Onassis, Vanessa
Redgrave, Diana Ross, Jean Seberg, Carly Simon, Barbra
Streisand, Elizabeth Taylor, Mary Tyler Moore, Natalie Wood

SPITTING IMAGE
who should play them in biopics? 25 suggestions

Errol Flynn (Kevin Kline)
Bette Davis (Susan Sarandon)
Paul Newman (Matthew McConaughey)
Marlene Dietrich (Madonna)
Stan Laurel (Clint Eastwood)
Brendan Behan (Chris Penn)
Ingrid Bergman (Isabella Rossellini)
Sidney Poitier (Denzel Washington)
Jerry Lewis (Jim Carrey)
Laurence Harvey (Keanu Reeves)
Rita Hayworth (Julia Roberts)
Grace Kelly (Gwyneth Paltrow)
James Dean (Brad Pitt)
Janet Leigh (Jamie Lee Curtis)
Richard Burton (Anthony Hopkins)

Vivien Leigh (Joanne Whalley-Kilmer)
John Gavin (Jason Patric)
William Bendix (John Goodman)
Vanessa Redgrave (Joely Richardson)
Judy Geeson (Cameron Diaz)
Tuesday Weld (Ashley Judd)
Marlon Brando (Ethan Hawke)
Elvis Presley (k.d. lang!)
Harrison Ford (Tim Matheson)
Lauren Bacall (Uma Thurman)

PORTRAIT OF THE ARTIST
10 stars who've played artists in biopics

David Bowie as Andy Warhol in *Basquiat* (1996)
Kirk Douglas as Vincent Van Gogh in *Lust for Life* (1956)
Anthony Quinn as Paul Gauguin in *Lust for Life* (1956)
Patrick Godfrey as Leonardo da Vinci in *Ever After* (1998)
Anthony Hopkins as Picasso in *Surviving Picasso* (1996)
Charles Laughton as Rembrandt in *Rembrandt* (1936)
Tim Roth as Vincent Van Gogh in *Vincent and Theo* (1990)
Joss Ackland as Matisse in *Surviving Picasso* (1996)
Derek Jacobi as Francis Bacon in *Love is the Devil* (1998)
Charlton Heston as Michelangelo in *The Agony and the Ecstasy* (1965)

STRANGER THAN FICTION
10 stars who've played writers in biopics

Gregory Peck as Ambrose Bierce in *Old Gringo* (1989)
Daniel Day-Lewis as Christy Brown in *My Left Foot* (1989)
Gregory Peck as F. Scott Fitzgerald in *Beloved Infidel* (1959)
Jack Nicholson as Eugene O'Neill in *Reds* (1981)
Vanessa Redgrave as Agatha Christie in *Agatha* (1978)
Olivia de Havilland as Charlotte Brontë in *Devotion* (1943)
Gary Oldman as Joe Orton in *Prick Up Your Ears* (1987)
Anthony Hopkins as C. S. Lewis in *Shadowlands* (1993)
Danny Kaye in *Hans Christian Andersen* (1952)
Johnny Depp as Hunter S. Thompson in *Fear and Loathing in Las Vegas* (1998)

SYMPHONY IN CELLULOID
10 stars who've played classical composers or musicians in biopics

Gary Oldman as Beethoven in *Immortal Beloved* (1994)
Mario Lanza as Enrico Caruso in *The Great Caruso* (1951)
Dirk Bogarde as Franz Liszt in *Song Without End* (1960)
Tom Hulce as Mozart in *Amadeus* (1984)
Richard Chamberlain as Tchaikovsky in *The Music Lovers* (1970)
Robert Powell as Mahler in *Mahler* (1974)
Luise Rainer as Strauss in *The Great Waltz* (1938)
Stewart Granger as violinist Paganini in *The Magic Bow* (1946)
Emily Watson as Jacqueline du Pré in *Hilary and Jackie* (1998)
Geoffrey Rush as David Helfgott in *Shine* (1996)

MOONLIGHTING
10 stars who appeared as other stars in biopics

Robert Downey, Jr. as Charlie Chaplin in *Chaplin* (1992)

Carroll Baker as Jean Harlow in *Harlow* (1965)

Jill Clayburgh as Carole Lombard in *Gable and Lombard* (1976)

James Brolin as Clark Gable in *Gable and Lombard* (1976)

Jessica Lange as Frances Farmer in *Frances* (1982)

Donald O'Connor as Keaton in *The Buster Keaton Story* (1957)

Rod Steiger as W. C. Fields in *W. C. Fields and Me* (1976)

Robert Sacchi as Bogey in *The Man with Bogart's Face* (1980)

Faye Dunaway as Joan Crawford in *Mommie Dearest* (1981)

Susan Hayward as Lillian Roth in *Animal Crackers* (1930)

WANDERIN' STARS
5 stars who changed their dates of birth

HUMPHREY BOGART
Born on January 14, 1899, but Warner Brothers claimed he was born on Christmas Day in order to romanticize his background.

JAMES CAGNEY
Born on July 17, 1899, the studio publicity department moved his birth year up to 1904 to capitalize on his baby-face appearance.

ROCK HUDSON
Actually born in 1925, but early in his career his agent added two years onto his age to secure more mature parts for him.

GENE HACKMAN
Born in 1931, he also added two years onto his age when he was 16 so that he could join the Marines.

ZSA ZSA GABOR
This lady is an Honors Graduate of the School of Creative
Economics when it comes to chronology, but it has been estab-
lished that she was born in 1919.

A STAR IS BORN
15 surprising birthplaces

Jessica Tandy (England), Olivia Hussey (Argentina),
Bela Lugosi (Transylvania), Basil Rathbone (South Africa),
Victoria Principal (Japan), Bob Hope (England), Merle Oberon
(Sri Lanka), Sam Neill (Ireland), Julie Christie (India),
Audrey Hepburn (Belgium), Elizabeth Taylor (England),
Simone Signoret (Germany), Edward G. Robinson (Bucharest),
Bruce Willis (Germany), Stan Laurel (England)

OH CANADA
10 stars who were born north of the border

Donald Sutherland, Norma Shearer, William Shatner,
Christopher Plummer, Walter Pidgeon, Mary Pickford, Barbara
Perkins, Raymond Massey, Michael J. Fox, Deanna Durbin

STAR-CROSSED
10 film folk who share identical dates of birth

Marlon Brando and Doris Day (April 3, 1924)
David Hemmings and Juliet Mills (November 21, 1941)
Meryl Streep and Lindsay Wagner (June 22, 1949)
Sylvester Stallone and Burt Ward (July 6, 1946)
Ben Kingsley and Sarah Miles (December 31, 1943)
Albert Finney and Glenda Jackson (May 9, 1936)
George Peppard and Laurence Harvey (October 1, 1928)
Karen Black and Genevieve Bujold (July 1, 1942)
Stephen Boyd and Gina Lollobrigida (July 4, 1928)
Jean-Luc Godard and Broderick Crawford (December 9, 1911)

IT'S A MAD, MAD WORLD
15 bizarre things that stars have done

EMILIO ESTEVEZ
Says that he's seen *Jaws* (1975) more than seventy times.

KENNETH WILLIAMS
Was so private he wouldn't even allow visitors to use his bathroom.

WARREN BEATTY
Claims to have memorized the complete works of Eugene O'Neill.

CECIL B. DE MILLE
A foot fetishist, he spent hours fondling the feet of his ingénues.

MADONNA
She once dyed her hair a different color every day of the week.

TONY CURTIS

At a première once he gave his automobile keys to the doorman and told him to keep the vehicle—he thought that was the hip thing to do.

LARRY HAGMAN

Has been known to celebrate American Independence Day by heading a parade along a beach in a gorilla skin, banging a drum.

JOHNNY DEPP

Tattooed "Winona Forever" on his arm when he was engaged to Winona Ryder. When their relationship broke up, he had some of the letters removed. It now reads, "Wino Forever."

ANTHONY QUINN

During his boxing years, he ran half a mile backwards every day.

DOLLY PARTON

Loves to buy fitness videos and then sit watching them while eating cookies.

SOPHIA LOREN

Derives great pleasure from rolling her bare feet over a wooden rolling pin while watching TV.

JAYNE MANSFIELD

Had practically everything in her house colored pink—including the water in her bathtub, which comprised pink champagne.

ROBERT REDFORD

Books whole rows of seats on plane trips so that he won't have to talk to other passengers.

CARY GRANT

Had a penchant for keeping buttons and assorted pieces of string.

HOWARD HUGHES

Toward the end of his life he kept all his urine in jars, which were always carefully labeled and cataloged.

OTHER THAN AL
10 stars who've blacked up on screen

Fred Astaire (*Swing Time*, 1935)
Dan Dailey (*You're My Everything*, 1949)
Flora Robson (*Saratoga Trunk*, 1945)
John Barrymore (*The Twentieth Century*, 1934)
Bing Crosby (*Dixie*, 1943)
Marion Davies (*Going Hollywood*, 1933)
Buster Keaton (*College*, 1927)
Gene Wilder (*Silver Streak*, 1976)
Betty Grable (*The Dolly Sisters*, 1945)
Judy Garland (*Ziegfeld Girl*, 1941)

TRADING PLACES
10 actresses who've used body doubles

Isabella Rossellini (*Death Becomes Her*, 1992)
Raquel Welch (*One Million Years B.C.*, 1966)
Geena Davis (*Thelma and Louise*, 1991)
Anne Archer (*Body of Evidence*, 1993)
Brooke Shields (*The Blue Lagoon*, 1980)
Kim Basinger (*My Stepmother is an Alien*, 1988)
Jennifer Beales (*Flashdance*, 1983)
Jane Fonda (*Coming Home*, 1978)
Julia Roberts (*Pretty Woman*, 1990)
Demi Moore (*Indecent Proposal*, 1993)

BOND IS BACK
10 Bond movie cliches

1. The blitzkrieg intro is probably going to be the best part of the movie.
2. The opening credits appear in a zany fashion, but you don't mind because there will probably be a nice song playing in the background.
3. In an early scene, Bond will act bored as M runs through the finer points of some ingenious gadget (the one you just know is going to save his skin an hour down the road).
4. When he's in bed with "Gorgeous Damsel," the lovemaking will usually be interrupted by the arrival of an unwanted intruder.
5. "Gorgeous Damsel" will very likely turn out to be a double agent who actually organized the arrival of the intruder to bump Bond off. (Bond will be hip to this, even if he appears to be more interested in getting into the Gorgeous Damsel's pants.)
6. Every time Bond fends off a crisis, he'll have a funny tag line, such as "Drop in again sometime," when he sends a villain hurtling through a roof.
7. When he inevitably gets captured, "Mr. Big" will tell him of his plans to change the world's weather, or something equally ridiculous.
8. There will be at least one big chase scene: by air, sea, and/or land. This will give Bond a chance to show his athletic skills. (And *still* not get that shirt dirty.)
9. Lots of people will die in the climactic scene.
10. Bond won't.

PAY ATTENTION, BOND
5 classic Bond gadgets

Goldfinger (1964)
Aston Martin DB5 with ejector seat, smoke-screen tanks, oil slicks, and a bulletproof shield.

License to Kill (1989)
Toothpaste tube with plastic explosives.

Live and Let Die (1973)
Electromagnetic watch with spinning blade.

The Spy Who Loved Me (1977)
Bond's Lotus Esprit doubles as a submarine, with missiles in the trunk, periscope, and radar.

The Living Daylights (1987)
The Aston Martin Volante has a rocket in the back of the car and skis for those bad weather problems.

PUSSY GALORE!
10 great Bond girl names

Ursula Andress as Honey Ryder in *Dr. No* (1962)
Honor Blackman as Pussy Galore in *Goldfinger* (1964)
Mie Hama as Kissy Suzuki in *You Only Live Twice* (1967)
Jill St. John as Tiffany Case in *Diamonds Are Forever* (1971)
Lana Wood as Plenty O'Toole in *Diamonds Are Forever* (1971)
Britt Ekland as Mary Goodnight in *Man with the Golden Gun* (1974)
Lois Chiles as Holly Goodhead in *Moonraker* (1979)
Maud Adams as Octopussy in *Octopussy* (1983)
Talisa Soto as Lupe Lamora in *License to Kill* (1989)
Famke Janssen as Xenia Onatopp in *Goldeneye* (1995)

RAGING BULLS
10 actors who've played boxers

Stacy Keach (*Fat City*, 1972)
Marlon Brando (*On The Waterfront*, 1954)
Daniel Day-Lewis (*The Boxer*, 1997)
Sylvester Stallone (*Rocky*, 1976)
Jon Voight (*The Champ*, 1979)
Robert de Niro (*Raging Bull*, 1980)
Paul Newman (*Somebody Up There Likes Me*, 1956)
Kirk Douglas (*Champion*, 1949)
Anthony Quinn (*Requiem for a Heavyweight*, 1962)
Robert Ryan (*The Set-Up*, 1949)

YOU MUST REMEMBER THIS
5 memorable lines from Casablanca

"Here's lookin' at you, kid."

"We'll always have Paris."

"The problems of three people don't amount to a hill of beans in this crazy world."

"This could be the beginning of a beautiful friendship."

"Of all the gin joints in all the world, she walked into mine."

BLINK AND YOU MISS 'EM
10 early cameo performances

JAMES WOODS in *The Way We Were* (1973)
Barbra Streisand's political activist university boyfriend.

RICHARD DREYFUSS in *The Graduate* (1967)
He only got one line: "Shall I get the cops? I'll get the cops."
Say no more.

JOHNNY DEPP in *Nightmare in Elm Street* (1984)
Thankless role as a teenager who doesn't want to fall asleep for fear of what Freddy Krueger might do. Can you blame him?

GEENA DAVIS in *Tootsie* (1982)
Briefly shares a dressing room with the cross-dressing Dustin "Dorothy" Hoffman.

JEFF GOLDBLUM in *Death Wish* (1974)
A forgettable mugger who falls prey to vigilante Charles
Bronson.

MICKEY ROURKE in *Body Heat* (1981)
The unscrupulous arsonist who gives William Hurt some advice.

HARRISON FORD in *Dead Heat on a Merry-Go-Round* (1966)
A bellboy with just one line of dialogue.

BRAD PITT in *Thelma and Louise* (1991)
The opportunistic hunk who makes out with Geena Davis and
then does a runner with her stash of cash.

SHARON STONE in *Stardust Memories* (1980)
Woody Allen's fantasy girl. She gives him an open-mouthed kiss
through the windows of a train carriage and then she's gone.

SIGOURNEY WEAVER in *Annie Hall* (1977)
"Unless you know my raincoat," Sigourney says, "you'll miss
me."

SEE NO EVIL, HEAR NO EVIL
15 examples of censorship

Belgium is the only country in the world which has never
imposed censorship on films for adults.

Denmark banished censorship for adult audiences in 1969,
followed by Austria and Portugal in the 1970s.

The word "Mafia" was totally deleted from the finished script
of *The Godfather* (1970) when the Italian-American League
brought pressure to bear on director Francis Ford Coppola.

C

Whiskey Galore (1949) had to be retitled *Tight Little Island* for the USA as the Hays Code prohibited the naming of alcoholic beverages.

Walt Disney had to cut a scene from *Snow White and the Seven Dwarfs* (1937) in which the little fellows were making up a bed for the eponymous lady. The Hays Code people felt that audiences might deduce that she was shacking up with them.

Mickey Mouse was once banned in Russia, Germany, and Italy .

Charlie Chaplin's *Limelight* (1952) was banned in the USA for twenty years because its politics were believed to be subversive.

Hitler once decreed that any female character who broke up a marriage in a film must die at the end.

Mussolini banned the Marx Brothers film *Duck Soup* (1933) in Italy because he felt that Groucho's Rufus T. Firefly resembled him too much. (Groucho, for his part, was rather pleased.)

Mike Nichols' *Carnal Knowledge* (1971), starring a sex-hungry Jack Nicholson and Art Garfunkel, was banned in Georgia in 1971 on the grounds that it was pornographic.

Elia Kazan's adaptation of Tennessee Williams' *Baby Doll* (1956) was condemned by the Catholic Legion of Decency for what it termed "carnal suggestiveness."

Biker classic *The Wild One* (1953), starring Marlon Brando, was banned in England for its violence. The ban wasn't lifted until fifteen years later, when it all started to look rather tame.

The James Dean classic *Rebel Without A Cause* (1955) was also banned in England upon its release. Moralists felt that its cult-of-youth overtones might encourage social unrest among the young.

The Blackboard Jungle (1955) was banned in Memphis and Georgia in 1955 for having the gall to feature a racially integrated classroom.

The King and I (1956) is still banned in Thailand, where it is seen as insulting and patronizing to Thai culture.

10 UNLIKELY VICTIMS OF CENSORSHIP

Invisible Agent (1942)
In one particular scene the eponymous agent takes a shower—the drops of water sticking to his skin are visible, but the skin itself isn't. The censors still banned it, however, because the bathroom door was open and there was a woman in the room beside it (who would, no doubt, have been corrupted by the liquid apparition).

From This Day Forward (1946)
In this RKO vehicle, a character remarks, "I didn't sleep well last night. It must have been those two cups of coffee I drank." The second sentence was deleted by RKO's advisor on foreign affairs for fear of offending Brazilian coffee-makers.

The Hypocrites (1915)
There was a nude scene in this movie, which the mayor of Boston handled in a rather messy fashion: he ordered clothes to be painted onto the girl's body frame by frame.

The Sunshine Boys (1975)
NBC took offense when Walter Matthau called George Burns a "putz," taking the word to denote "penis" rather than the more common understanding of "jerk."

Silkwood (1983)
The Mexican censor cut the parts where Cher expresses her character's lesbian tendencies.

Madame Butterfly (1932)
Japan cut a scene because it featured (horror of horrors) Sylvia Sidney's left elbow in all its nakedness as she was being embraced by Cary Grant.

The Outlaw (1943)
Censored because Jane Russell's mammary endowments were regarded as unacceptable.

Going My Way (1944)
This was banned in many Latin American countries in the 1940s because Bing Crosby's priest was featured in it wearing a sweat-shirt and baseball cap.

Treasure Island (1920)
Ohio's Censorship Board tried to ban this, fearing that it would incite children to become pirates in later life.

Birth of a Nation (1915)
Denver cinema manager Robert E. Allen was sentenced to 120 days in jail in 1939 for showing D. W. Griffiths' masterpiece—because he was alleged to have flouted a city ordinance that prohibited the exhibition of motion pictures that were calculated either to stir up racial prejudice or to disturb the peace.

PLAY IT AGAIN SAM
the 20 most–portrayed characters on screen

Sherlock Holmes (211 times)
Napoleon (194)
Dracula (161)
Frankenstein (159)
Abraham Lincoln (137)
Tarzan (99)
Cinderella (95)
Zorro (70)
Hopalong Cassidy (66)
The Durango kid (64)
Robin Hood (59)
Buffalo Bill (53)
Ulysses S. Grant (50)
Charlie Chan (49)
Billy the Kid (49)
George Washington (38)
Jesse James (38)
Wild Bill Hickok (37)
General George Custer (33)
Wyatt Earp (25)

5 FAMOUS REAL-LIFE CHARACTERS PORTRAYED BY TWO DIFFERENT STARS

RUDOLPH VALENTINO
Gene Wilder (*The World's Greatest Lover*, 1977)
Rudolf Nureyev (*Valentino*, 1977)

MOSES
Burt Lancaster (*Moses*, 1975)
Charlton Heston (*The Ten Commandments*, 1956)

BABE RUTH
William Bendix (*The Babe Ruth Story*, 1948)
John Goodman (*Babe*, 1992)

SALLY BOWLES
Julie Harris (*I Am a Camera*, 1955)
Liza Minnelli (*Cabaret*, 1972)

AL CAPONE
Rod Steiger (*Al Capone*, 1959)
Robert de Niro (*The Untouchables*, 1987)

5 FAMOUS FICTIONAL CHARACTERS PORTRAYED BY TWO DIFFERENT STARS

THE HUNCHBACK OF NOTRE DAME
Charles Laughton (*The Hunchback of Notre Dame*, 1939)
Anthony Quinn (*The Hunchback of Notre Dame*, 1957)

CAPTAIN AHAB
John Barrymore (*Moby Dick*, 1930)
Gregory Peck (*Moby Dick*, 1956)

TOM JONES
Albert Finney (*Tom Jones*, 1963)
Nicky Henson (*The Bawdy Adventures of Tom Jones*, 1976)

ROBINSON CRUSOE
Aidan Quinn (*Crusoe*, 1988)
Dan O'Herlihy (*The Adventures of Robinson Crusoe*, 1952)

DOROTHY
Judy Garland (*The Wizard of Oz*, 1939)
Diana Ross (*The Wiz*, 1978)

TERMS OF ENDEARMENT
20 on-screen come-ons

"You know the sort of girl who doesn't sleep with a man on a first date? Well I'm not one of those." (Emma Thompson to Jeff Goldblum in *The Tall Guy*, 1990)

"Well, Max, here we are: middle-aged man reaffirming his middle-aged manhood and a terrified young woman with a father complex. What sort of script do you think we can make out of this?" (Faye Dunaway to William Holden in *Network*, 1976)

"Get me a man and I'll marry him. Anything, as long as it's got pants." (Lee Grant gets desperate in *Detective Story*, 1951)

"I've arrived at the age where a platonic relationship can be sustained on the highest moral plane." (Charlie Chaplin to Claire Bloom in *Limelight*, 1952)

"Let's get married and if that doesn't work out we'll live together and if that doesn't work out we'll date." (Randy Quaid in *Lightning*, 1996)

"Don't you think it's better for a girl to be preoccupied with sex than occupied?" (Maggie McNamara in *The Moon is Blue*, 1953)

"That was the most fun I've had without laughing." (Woody Allen to Diane Keaton after coitus in *Annie Hall*, 1977)

"I used to live like Robinson Crusoe, shipwrecked among eight million people. Then one day I saw a footprint in the sand, and there you were." (Jack Lemmon to Shirley MacLaine in *The Apartment*, 1960)

C

"You're the most beautiful woman I've ever seen, which doesn't say much for you." (Groucho Marx in *Duck Soup*, 1933)

"Why don't you get a divorce and settle down?" (Oscar Levant to Joan Crawford in *Humoresque*, 1946)

"Your idea of fidelity is not having more than one man in bed at the same time." (Dirk Bogarde to Julie Christie in *Darling*, 1965)

"If you come upstairs you're gonna get laid." (Christine Taylor to Adam Sandler in *The Wedding Singer*, 1998)

"Well I'll tell you the truth now. I ain't a real cowboy, but I'm one helluva stud." (Jon Voight selling his wares in *Midnight Cowboy*, 1969)

"I suppose you know you have a wonderful body. I'd like to do it in clay." (Lola Albright to Kirk Douglas in *Champion*, 1949)

"Why don't you get out of that wet coat and into a dry martini?" (Robert Benchley to Ginger Rogers in *The Major and the Minor*, 1942)

"How about coming up to my place for a spot of heavy breathing?" (Walter Matthau to Carol Burnett in *Pete 'n' Tillie*, 1972)

"Will you marry me? I'm aging visibly." (Raymond Massey to Joan Crawford in *Possessed*, 1947)

"Come to my room in half an hour and bring me some rye bread." (Jimmy Durante to Mary Wickes in *The Man Who Came to Dinner*, 1941)

"You'll never want for food and you'll never worry about rent. I've got good teeth and I'm not tattooed." (Richard Todd issues an unorthodox marriage proposal to Patricia Neal in *The Hasty Heart*, 1949)

"That's a honey of an anklet you're wearing, Mrs. Dietrichson." (Fred McMurray to Barbara Stanwyck in *Double Indemnity*, 1944)

BOUND FOR GLORY
10 child stars who also made it as adult stars

James Fox
Roddy McDowall
Mickey Rooney
Sammy Davis, Jr.
Ethan Hawke

Elizabeth Taylor
Jodie Foster
Judy Garland
Mary Pickford
Drew Barrymore

10 WHO FAILED TO MAKE THE GRADE

Macaulay Culkin
Jack Wild
Anthony Newley
Tommy Rettig
Justin Henry

Geraldine Chaplin
Pamela Franklin
Hayley Mills
Tatum O'Neal
Shirley Temple

MINORITY RULES
10 stars' children who made it themselves

CARRIE FISHER
Daughter of Debbie Reynolds and Eddie Fisher

MIA FARROW
Daughter of Maureen O'Sullivan

EMILIO ESTEVEZ and CHARLIE SHEEN
Sons of Martin Sheen

LIZA MINNELLI
Daughter of Judy Garland and Vincente Minnelli

MICHAEL DOUGLAS
Son of Kirk Douglas

JAMIE LEE CURTIS
Daughter of Tony Curtis and Janet Leigh

JEFF and BEAU BRIDGES
Sons of Lloyd Bridges

VANESSA REDGRAVE
Daughter of Michael and mother of Natasha and Joely
Richardson

JANE and PETER FONDA
Children of Henry Fonda

BRIDGET FONDA
Daughter of Peter Fonda

TICKETS PLEASE
5 odd facts about movie theaters

1. Some early American movie theaters provided day care, reading rooms, and even the services of a podiatrist.
2. In the late 1920s, the Roxy in New York had a hospital, a ballet troupe, and a hundred-strong choir.
3. Author James Joyce was Ireland's first movie theater manager.
4. A theater in Atlanta has been showing *Gone with the Wind* (1939) twice a day every day since it opened.
5. There's a theater in Iceland which seats just seventeen people.

LONG TIME NO SEE
10 star comebacks

PETER FONDA
Oscar-nominated performance in *Ulee's Gold* (1997) after being in every turkey you'd care to mention since the wild (but short-lived) fame consequent on *Easy Rider* (1969).

JOHN TRAVOLTA
Megafame (again) after Quentin Tarantino plucked him from the celluloid doldrums for *Pulp Fiction* (1994). "I started making comebacks", the former disco king once said, "when I was twenty-four."

MARLON BRANDO
Actually took a screen test for *The Godfather* (1972), being box-office poison by then as the result of a decade characterized by bad career choices, spiraling movie budgets, irrational behavior both on and off movie sets, and making many films purely to pay alimony to his many ex'es.

C

GLORIA SWANSON
Assembly-line cameo in *Airport '75* (1974) after her "swansong" performance in *Mio Figlio Nerone* (1956) eighteen years before.

GEORGE BURNS
Got an Oscar for *The Sunshine Boys* (1975) at the tender age of 80, having been absent from the screen since 1939.

MAE WEST
Chose Gore Vidal's camp sex-change vehicle *Myra Breckinridge* (1970) for her gala return to the big screen after an absence of thirty-five years.

JAMES CAGNEY
Cameoed in Milos Forman's *Ragtime* (1981), having been in retirement for twenty years previously. His doctor advised him to tread the boards again in order that he would live longer. Apparently, he was right.

AUDREY HEPBURN
Did a Garbo from the movies after *Robin and Marian* (1976), feeling they were obsessed with sex and violence, but Steven Spielberg persuaded her to do a gentle cameo in *Always* (1989).

FRANK SINATRA
Secured the role of Maggio in *From Here to Eternity* (1953) against all the odds, doing it for a paltry $8,000. He won an Oscar for the part and never really looked back afterward.

BURT REYNOLDS
Got an Oscar nomination for playing the seedy pornographic filmmaker in *Boogie Nights* (1998), after years of doing straight-to-video pulp and TV sitcoms.

GAME FOR A LAUGH
10 (usually) serious stars do comedy

Arnold Schwarzenneger (*Kindergarten Cop*, 1990)
Sylvester Stallone (*Stop or My Mom Will Shoot*, 1992)
Robert de Niro (*Midnight Run*, 1988)
Paul Newman (*The Life and Times of Judge Roy Bean*, 1972)
Clint Eastwood (*Bronco Billy*, 1980)
Lee Marvin (*Cat Ballou*, 1965)
Kirk Douglas (*Tough Guys*, 1986)
Steve McQueen (*The Reivers*, 1969)
Dustin Hoffman (*Tootsie*, 1982)
Marlon Brando (*Bedtime Story*, 1963)

AND VICE VERSA...
10 comedy stars in serious roles

Steve Martin (*Grand Canyon*, 1991)
Charlie Chaplin (*Monsieur Verdoux*, 1947)
Peter Sellers (*Being There*, 1979)
Don Rickles (*Casino*, 1995)
Robin Williams (*Dead Poets Society*, 1989)
Whoopi Goldberg (*The Color Purple*, 1985)
Goldie Hawn (*Deceived*, 1991)
Jerry Lewis (*King of Comedy*, 1982)
Jim Carrey (*The Truman Show*, 1998)
Woody Allen (*The Front*, 1976)

STAND AND DELIVER
10 stars who started as stand-up comedians

Robin Williams, Eddie Murphy, Steve Martin, Woody Allen, Billy Crystal, Jim Carrey, Mike Myers, Jerry Seinfeld, Rowan Atkinson, Billy Connolly

FROM PAGE TO STAGE
15 stars who've played comic–strip characters

Christopher Reeve (*Superman*), John Goodman (*Fred Flintstone*),
Jack Nicholson (*The Joker*), Michael Keaton (*Batman*),
Gene Hackman (*Lex Luthor*), Sylvester Stallone (*Judge Dredd*),
Nicholas Hammond (*Spiderman*), Helen Slater (*Supergirl*),
Robin Williams (*Popeye*), Warren Beatty (*Dick Tracy*),
Michelle Pfeiffer (*Catwoman*), Al Pacino (*Big Boy Caprice*),
Jim Carrey (*The Riddler*), Danny de Vito (*The Penguin*),
Billy Zane (*The Phantom*)

THE GANG'S ALL HERE
5 stars who played alongside cartoon characters

BOB HOSKINS (*Who Framed Roger Rabbit*, 1988)
Bob falls for animated amour Jessica Rabbit.

GENE KELLY (*Anchors Aweigh*, 1944)
Tap-dancing with Jerry of *Tom and Jerry* fame.

ANGELA LANSBURY (*Bedknobs and Broomsticks*, 1971)
Lansbury et al. referee a game of soccer and can be found
"bobbing along on the bottom of the beautiful briny sea."

JULIE ANDREWS (*Mary Poppins*, 1964)
Andrews dances with penguins, wins a horse race and warbles
with Cockneys. Practically perfect in every way.

MICHAEL JORDAN (*Space Jam*, 1996)
Shooting hoops with Bugs and co.

SHE'S GOTTA HAVE IT
15 contractual stipulations

LUCILLE BALL
Her contract had one unusual stipulation: that she always
remained twenty pounds overweight.

MAE WEST
Had it written into her contract that nobody would wear white on
the sets of her films. (This Snow White drifted—remember?)

BUD ABBOTT and LOU COSTELLO
Had an insurance clause against anyone who died laughing at
any of their movies.

SPENCER TRACY
Asked once what was the main thing that he looked for in a
contract, he replied, "Days off."

TONY CURTIS
Claimed to have had a "kissing clause" in his contracts, which
allowed him to canoodle his female costars.

SHIRLEY TEMPLE
Had a clause written into her contract that her hair always had to have fifty-six little curls in it when she appeared in front of the cameras.

TREVOR HOWARD
Had it written into his contract that he couldn't be called on to work on any day that the English team were playing cricket.

SIOBHÁN McKENNA
After she played Our Lady in *King of Kings* (1961), she had to sign a contract saying that she wouldn't be involved in a divorce for five years.

JOHN BARRYMORE
A notorious late-night drinker, Barrymore's contracts stipulated he wouldn't start work before 10.30 in the morning.

ELIZABETH TAYLOR
In her heyday, she was alleged to be so much the property of MGM that nothing except illness happened to her by accident.

EVELYN VENABLES
Had a clause in her contract insisting that she should not be kissed on screen. (She wouldn't really have got on with Tony Curtis, would she?)

BUSTER KEATON
His MGM contract banned him from smiling on screen and thus ruining his "Old Stoneface" image.

JOE E. BROWN
His contract forbade him to be seen on screen with a moustache.

JOAN CRAWFORD
Her 1933 contract with MGM was so detailed (and stringent) it even had a clause in it stipulating what time she was expected to be in bed each night.

GOLDIE HAWN

Insisted on an unusual clause in her movie contract in 1998: that her behind had to be repeatedly on display for any film she decided to do.

LOVE IN THE AFTERNOON
5 affairs Gary Cooper conducted on the sets of his movies

Clara Bow, during the making of *It* (1927)
Helen Hayes, while making *A Farewell to Arms* (1932)
Marlene Dietrich, his costar in *Desire* (1936)
Ingrid Bergman, on the set of *Saratoga Trunk* (1945)
Patricia Neal, his costar in *The Fountainhead* (1949)

FATAL ATTRACTIONS
10 cuckoo-in-the-nest movies

Unlawful Entry (1992)
Crazy cop Ray Liotta weans himself into the confidence of yuppie suburban couple Kurt Russell and Madeleine Stowe before going ape.

The Hand that Rocks the Cradle (1992)
Rebecca de Mornay can't have a baby, so she decides to be a nanny to Annabella Sciorra's one instead. This, alas, entails a bit of murder, husband-snatching, and whatnot.

C

Single White Female (1992)
Dysfunctional Jennifer Jason Leigh would like some company,
so she targets roommate-seeking Bridget Fonda. Copycat mania
ensues.

The Stepfather (1987)
Terry O'Quinn just can't seem to set down roots anywhere
because, just as he's got a new wife and life on the go, dammit,
some upstart from the past wants to expose him. Such individuals
must doubtless be liquidated pronto as a huge threat to Family
Values.

Fatal Attraction (1987)
Michael Douglas has a one-night stand with lonely Glenn Close.
Or so he thinks. She wants to get, er, closer. So, does he tell
loyal wife Anne Archer or risk having his rabbit stewed?

Consenting Adults (1992)
Kevin Kline falls for Ye Olde Wife-Swapping Trick and discovers that his neighbor Kevin Spacey isn't quite as neighborly as
he imagined. Oh, and Mary Elizabeth Mastrantonio (his
betrothed) is also in on the act.

The Devil's Own (1997)
Decent Irish-American cop Harrison Ford takes in a relative
from Northern Ireland (Brad Pitt) whose soft charm conceals the
fact that he wants to blow the Brits to bits. Lovely Donegal
accent, however.

The Servant (1963)
Dirk Bogarde is the manservant from hell, as he fights his own
particular class war with boss James Fox. Classic role-reversal
chiller.

Pacific Heights (1990)
When Melanie Griffith and Matthew Modine decide to let their luxury apartment to Michael Keaton, he takes certain liberties with your average landlord/tenant relationship (for instance, scaring the living Jesus out of the pair of them).

The Temp (1993)
A secretary with major ambitions (most of them unfulfilled) goes a little over the top in her attempts to secure that all-important promotion. Cue lots of body bags among the filofaxes.

D

THE BIG SLEEP
10 deathly phenomena

CHARLIE CHAPLIN
His body was stolen from its grave in Switzerland in 1977 and
held for ransom by a group of men who said that they needed the
money to start up a garage business.

SOPHIA LOREN
Believes that, after her grandmother died, her spirit entered her
own body.

DAVID JANSSEN
Had a dream forty-eight hours before his death (aged 49) in
which his coffin was being carried out of his house.

OLIVER REED
Left £10,000 out of his estate for his friends, so that they could
have a drinking spree at his funeral.

MADONNA
Has bought a burial plot beside Marilyn Monroe's so that they
can be together forever after she dies.

MONTGOMERY CLIFT
They say his ghost roams round the Hollywood Roosevelt
Hotel playing a bugle (as a nod to his *From Here to Eternity*
character).

HARRY COHN
His (many) enemies used to say, "You had to stand in line to
hate him." After he died in 1958 and drew a large crowd at his
funeral, Red Skelton quipped, "It just goes to show you: give the
public what they want and they'll turn out for it."

ELVIS PRESLEY
It's often been said that dying, for Elvis, was a brilliant career move: he was almost bankrupt when he passed away and his estate is now worth many more millions than it was when he was alive.

HUMPHREY BOGART
After he died, Lauren Bacall, his widow, put a gold whistle in his coffin in remembrance of the famous scene in *To Have and Have Not* (1945) in which she flirts seductively with him using this motif.

JOHN BARRYMORE
When he was on his deathbed, the priest asked him if he had anything to confess. Barrymore looked over his shoulder at the pretty nurse in attendance and said, "Yes, Father. Carnal thoughts about the lady behind you."

FOREVER YOUNG
10 stars who died before their time

SAL MINEO
Stabbed to death in an alleyway in 1976 for an unknown motive —no money was taken from his wallet. He was 37.

VIVIEN LEIGH
Died at the age of 54 from tuberculosis.

VERONICA LAKE
Died, also aged 54, from hepatitis.

JEFF CHANDLER
Got blood poisoning after surgery for a slipped disk and died in hospital aged 43.

D

JEAN HARLOW
Died aged 26 from complications arising from a bladder infection. (She refused medical attention because it conflicted with her Christian Science beliefs.)

GEORGE REEVES
Was found dead in his bedroom in June 1959, after being shot in the head. Controversy still surrounds the circumstances, and many people believe, not that he committed suicide, but that he was murdered. He was 45 years old.

RUDOLPH VALENTINO
When he passed away in 1926, from complications following a gastric ulcer and a ruptured appendix, several women committed suicide at the loss of their love god at the tender age of 31.

LUPE VELEZ
The so-called Mexican Spitfire tried to end her turbulent life at 36 in 1934 by overdosing on sleeping pills. She under-estimated the dosage, however, and, feeling violently sick, made a dash for the bathroom. On the way, she slipped and was flung head first into the toiletbowl and drowned.

ELVIS PRESLEY
Died on his toilet at Graceland at the age of 42. The autopsy showed more than a dozen different chemical substances in his body.

WALLACE REID
Died in a sanatorium aged 30 after an all-too-short life spent largely trying to kick a drug habit.

FROM HERE TO ETERNITY
5 decidedly untimely deaths

PETER LORRE
Died just half an hour before he was due in a divorce court.

INGRID BERGMAN
Died on her sixty-seventh birthday in 1982.

PETER WEILLER
In 1994 this German movie-goer was savagely beaten to death by ushers because he had brought his own popcorn.

JUDY GARLAND
Like Elvis Presley, she died on the toilet.

W. C. FIELDS
He always hated Christmas Day, so perhaps it was fitting that he actually died on December 25.

WE'LL MEET AGAIN
5 pairs of stars who died on the same day and year as other entertainers

Orson Welles and Yul Brynner (October 10, 1985)
Zeppo Marx and Joyce Grenfell (November 30, 1979)
River Phoenix and Federico Fellini (October 31, 1993)
David Niven and Raymond Massey (July 29, 1983)
Klaus Kinski and Freddie Mercury (November 24, 1991)

THEY DIED WITH THEIR BOOTS ON
10 stars who died in mid-shoot

Bill Mead died on the set of this very movie (i.e. *They Died With Their Boots On*, 1941), when riding opposite Errol Flynn. His horse threw him, and, though he had the presence of mind to throw his sword forward to avoid falling on it, it stuck in the ground hilt-down and he impaled himself on it.

Tyrone Power and his father (who had the same Christian name) both died on film sets, in 1959 and 1932 respectively.

Jean Harlow died during the making of *Saratoga* (1937). (A double stood in for her and the film was completed.)

John Candy died at the age of 42 during the making of *Wagons East* (1994), after a history of health problems resulting from his gross obesity.

River Phoenix was in mid-shoot with *Dark Blood* when a lethal cocktail of cocaine and heroin caused his death in Johnny Depp's Viper Room nightclub in 1993.

Brandon Lee, the son of martial arts guru Bruce, was accidentally shot to death during the making of *The Crow* (1994), when a real bullet was used in a scene instead of a blank.

Marilyn Monroe died when she was making the aptly titled *Something's Got to Give* (1962). The film was never completed. She had been sacked from the production before her death due to repeated absenteeism from the set for little apparent reason. It was only in the aftermath of her Nembutal overdose that people realized how deep her depression went.

Anthony Perkins died of AIDS during the making of *Psycho V* (1992), the fifth movie of the series that made him famous.

Robert Walker died from a medically induced drug trauma during the filming of *My Son John* (1952).

Oliver Reed died in 1999, aged 61, in a pub in Malta during the making of Ridley Scott's *The Gladiator.*

THE LAST PICTURE SHOW
5 stars who died soon after finishing movies

CLARK GABLE
Twelve days after finishing *The Misfits* (1961).

SPENCER TRACY
Fifteen days after completing *Guess Who's Coming To Dinner* (1967).

JAMES DEAN
Two days after *Giant* wrapped (1955).

HENRY FONDA
Shortly after a moving farewell (and screen reconciliation with the erstwhile-alienated Jane) in *On Golden Pond* (1981).

PETER FINCH
After finishing *Network* (1977), but before the Oscars (he had been nominated) were announced. He was given the first posthumous one.

THE ONLY WAY IS UP
10 inauspicious debuts

SYLVESTER STALLONE
As a subway mugger in Woody Allen's *Bananas* (1971).

JODIE FOSTER
At the age of 3 in a TV commercial.

JAMES DEAN
In a Pepsi commercial.

CHARLES BRONSON
In the film *You're in the Army Now* (1950) "because I proved I could belch on cue."

JOHN TRAVOLTA
In a schlocky shocker about Satanists called *The Devil's Rain* (1975).

JOHN FORD
As an extra in the Ku Klux Klan in D. W. Griffiths' *Birth of a Nation* (1915).

SPENCER TRACY
Playing a robot in a Broadway show called *Are You There?*

RICHARD DREYFUSS
Had a one-liner as a college kid in *The Graduate* (1967).

MICHAEL CAINE
Played a robot in his first role and earned this commendation from a South London critic: "As a robot, Mr. Caine was very convincing."

CLINT EASTWOOD
As a lab technician in the cheap horror flick *Revenge of the Creature* (1955).

BEGINNER'S LUCK?

5 actors nominated for Oscars on their debuts

Orson Welles (*Citizen Kane*, 1941)
Montgomery Clift (*The Search*, 1948)
Richard Widmark (*Kiss of Death*, 1947)
Terence Stamp (*Billy Budd*, 1962)
Jack Wild (*Oliver*, 1968)

10 ACTRESSES NOMINATED FOR OSCARS ON THEIR DEBUTS

Marlee Matlin (*Children of a Lesser God*, 1986)
Julie Andrews (*Mary Poppins*, 1964)
Barbra Streisand (*Funny Girl*, 1968)
Diana Ross (*Lady Sings the Blues*, 1972)
Julie Walters (*Educating Rita*, 1983)
Whoopi Goldberg (*The Color Purple*, 1985)
Tatum O'Neal (*Paper Moon*, 1973)
Glenn Close (*The World According to Garp*, 1982)
Audrey Hepburn (*Roman Holiday*, 1953)
Estelle Parsons (*Bonnie and Clyde*, 1967)

METHOD TO HIS MADNESS
Robert De Niro: 10 preparations

To get into the part of Al Capone in *The Untouchables* (1987), he had a tailor make him identical pairs of the kind of silk underwear that Capone liked to wear.

He hung around with bounty hunters to prepare himself for playing one in *Midnight Run* (1988)—even making some arrests in the process.

He learned the entire Latin Mass by heart before he played a priest in *True Confessions* (1981).

He wore an incontinence diaper during the shooting of *Awakenings* (1990) to understand his character better, a man who emerges from a catatonic state with the help of pioneering drug treatment.

During the shooting of *King of Comedy* (1983), he refused to have dinner with his costar Jerry Lewis because his character in the movie wouldn't have done so.

He studied videotapes and tape recordings of people who were dyslexic in order to get into the part of the illiterate blue-collar cook that he played in *Stanley and Iris* (1990).

He learned to play the sax for *New York, New York* (1977), throwing himself into the production with such zeal that, after the climactic fight scene with Liza Minnelli, he ended up in a hospital emergency room—along with Minnelli and director Martin Scorsese.

He put on sixty pounds to play boxer Jake La Motta in *Raging Bull* (1980), eating his way around Italy in a manner that caused him deep depression. (The depression worsened when he had to get rid of the weight after the film wrapped.)

One scene in *Once Upon A Time in America* (1984), in which he had to wake up to the sound of an alarm clock, had to be shot over twenty times. He insisted on a different clock being provided each time so that he could register genuine surprise.

In *Bloody Mama* (1970), where he played a guy who had to deteriorate physically, co-star Shelley Winters commented, "His face got this horribly chalky look and his skin broke out in disgusting sores. I don't think he ate a bite of food during the entire shooting of the movie."

ARE YOU TALKIN' TO ME?
De Niro's 10 most famous roles

JON RUBIN (*Hi Mom!*, 1970)
Blue movie-maker who does things like tip TV sets over and fire bullets at them.

JOHNNY BOY (*Mean Streets*, 1973)
Manic ball of energy in New York's Little Italy.

TRAVIS BICKLE (*Taxi Driver*, 1976)
Dysfunctional Vietnam vet who shoots up half of New York and tries to reform neophyte hooker Jodie Foster.

JAKE LA MOTTA (*Raging Bull*, 1980)
Loopy slugger who forgets that he's not in a boxing ring when he gets angry with his wife or brother.

NOODLES (*Once Upon a Time in America*, 1984)
Killer, rapist, stooge.

HARRY TUTTLE (*Brazil*, 1985)
Spaced-out air-conditioning repairman.

JIMMY THE GENT (*Goodfellas*, 1990)
Ruthless mobster.

ACE ROTHSTEIN (*Casino*, 1995)
Casino manager with underworld connections.

MAX CADY (*Cape Fear*, 1991)
Tattoo-clad, Bible-spoutin' bad ole boy intent on revenge for
years spent in the clink.

RUPERT PUPKIN (*King of Comedy*, 1982)
Deranged and obsessive talk-show-host stalker.

HERE'S LOOKIN' AT YOU, KID
10 descriptions of stars

MAGGIE SMITH
"Quentin Crisp in drag" James Coco

BASIL RATHBONE
"Two profiles pasted together" Dorothy Parker

AUDREY HEPBURN
"Patron saint of the anorexics" Orson Welles

PAUL NEWMAN
"A great-looking ice cube" Sal Mineo

GLENDA JACKSON
"A face to launch a thousand dredgers" Jack de Manio

CLARK GABLE
"The best ears of our lives" Bob Hope

JOAN COLLINS
"Someone who looks like she combs her hair with an eggbeater"
Hedda Hopper

JEREMY IRONS
"An iceberg with an accent" Andy Warhol

BARBRA STREISAND
"A cross between an aardvark and an albino rat, surmounted by a
platinum-coated horse bun" John Simon

DANNY DE VITO
"A coarse, out-of-shape pea who has accidentally left the pod
and gone for a walk" John Peters

JUST WHEN YOU THOUGHT IT WAS SAFE...
5 things films deterred us from doing

Jaws (1975)
Swimming anywhere near a beach where Roy Scheider looks
worried.

Single White Female (1992)
Allowing roommates to copy our hairdo.

Fatal Attraction (1987)
Sleeping with women who don't wash their dishes.

Falling Down (1993)
Complaining about traffic jams.

The Godfather (1972)
Going to bed without double-checking the sheets.

THE DEVIL RIDES OUT
10 actors who've played Old Nick

Walter Huston (*All That Money Can Buy*, 1941)
Ray Milland (*Alias Nick Beal*, 1949)
Yves Montand (*Marguerite of the Night*, 1956)
Vincent Price (*The Story of Mankind*, 1957)
Lon Chaney (*The Devil's Messenger*, 1962)
Donald Pleasence (*The Greatest Story Ever Told*, 1965)
Burgess Meredith (*The Sentinel*, 1977)
Simon Ward (*Holocaust 2000*, 1978)
Robert De Niro (*Angel Heart*, 1987)
Al Pacino (*The Devil's Advocate*, 1997)

TELL IT LIKE IT IS
10 classic film noir lines

"You know something? You're a pretty nice guy—for a girl."
(Robert Mitchum to Jean Simmons in *Angel Face*, 1953)

"Life in Loyaltown is like sitting in a funeral parlor waiting for the funeral to begin."
(Bette Davis in *Beyond the Forest*, 1949)

"He's dead now, except he's breathing."
(Edmund O'Brien in *The Killers)*

"Live fast, die young and make a good-looking corpse."
(John Derek in *Knock on Any Door*, 1949)

"I've been rich and I've been poor. Believe me, rich is better."
(Gloria Grahame in *The Big Heat*, 1953)

"I probably shan't return before dawn. How I detest the dawn. The grass looks likes it's been out all night."
(Clifton Webb in *The Dark Corner*, 1946)

"They say native Californians all come from Iowa."
(Fred MacMurray in *Double Indemnity*, 1944)

"If I'd been a ranch, they would have named me the Bar Nothing."
(Rita Hayworth in *Gilda*, 1946)

"When I have nothing to do at night and can't think, I always iron my money."
(Robert Mitchum in *His Kind of Woman*, 1951)

"Be smart, Charlie. Act dumb."
(Gangster boss to Forrest Tucker in *Hoodlum Empire*, 1952)

DIRECTOR'S CUT
20 directors who appeared in their own films

Francis Ford Coppola (*Apocalypse Now*, 1979)
Sydney Pollack (*Tootsie*, 1982)
Preston Sturges (*Paris Holiday*, 1958)
Mitchell Leisen (*Hold Back the Dawn*, 1941)
Nicholas Ray (*55 Days in Peking*, 1963)
Jules Dassin (*Rififi*, 1954)
Hugo Fregonese (*Decameron Nights*, 1953)
Sam Fuller (*House of Bamboo*, 1955)
Tony Richardson (*Tom Jones*, 1963)
Michael Winner (*You Must Be Joking*, 1965)
King Vidor (*Our Daily Bread*, 1934)
Joseph Losey (*The Intimate Stranger*, 1956)
Cecil B. De Mille (*Sunset Boulevard*, 1950)
Robert Aldrich (*The Big Knife*, 1955)
John Huston (*The Bible*, 1966)
Paul Mazursky (*Blume in Love*, 1973)
Quentin Tarantino (*Pulp Fiction*, 1994)
François Truffaut (*Day for Night*, 1973)
Martin Scorsese (*Taxi Driver*, 1976)
Roman Polanski (*Chinatown*, 1974)

THE USUAL SUSPECTS

10 directors who repeatedly used the same stars

MARTIN SCORSESE
Worked with ROBERT DE NIRO on:
Taxi Driver (1976), *New York, New York* (1977), *Raging Bull* (1980), *King of Comedy* (1982), *Goodfellas* (1990), *Cape Fear* (1992), *Casino* (1995)

ROGER CORMAN
Worked with JACK NICHOLSON on:
Cry Baby Killer (1958), *Little Shop of Horrors* (1960), *The Raven* (1963), *The Terror* (1963), *The St. Valentine's Day Massacre* (1967), *The Trip* (1967)

ANTHONY MANN
Worked with JAMES STEWART on:
Winchester 73 (1950), *Bend of the River* (1952), *The Naked Spur* (1953), *The Glenn Miller Story* (1953), *The Far Country* (1955), *The Man from Laramie* (1955)

JOHN FORD
Worked with JOHN WAYNE on:
Stagecoach (1939), *The Long Voyage Home* (1940), *They Were Expendable* (1945), *Fort Apache* (1948), *She Wore a Yellow Ribbon* (1949), *Rio Grande* (1950), *The Quiet Man* (1952), *The Searchers* (1956), *The Wings of Eagles* (1957), *The Horse Soldiers* (1959), *How the West Was Won* (1962), *The Man Who Shot Liberty Valance* (1962), *Donovan's Reef* (1963)

SYDNEY POLLACK
Worked with ROBERT REDFORD on:
This Property is Condemned (1966), *Jeremiah Johnson* (1972), *The Way We Were* (1973), *Three Days of the Condor* (1975), *The Electric Horseman* (1979), *Out of Africa* (1985)

ROBERT ALTMAN
Worked with SHELLEY DUVALL on:
Brewster McCloud (1970), *McCabe and Mrs. Miller* (1971), *Thieves Like Us* (1974), *Nashville* (1975), *Buffalo Bill and the Indians* (1976), *Three Women* (1977)

ALFRED HITCHCOCK
Worked with JAMES STEWART on:
Rope (1948), *Rear Window* (1954), *The Man Who Knew Too Much* (1956), *Vertigo* (1958)

BILLY WILDER
Worked with JACK LEMMON on:
Some Like it Hot (1959), *The Apartment* (1960), *Irma La Douce* (1963), *The Fortune Cookie* (1966), *The Front Page* (1974)

JOHN FRANKENHEIMER
Worked with BURT LANCASTER on:
The Young Savages (1961), *The Birdman of Alcatraz* (1962), *Seven Days in May* (1964), *The Train* (1964), *The Gypsy Moths* (1970)

INGMAR BERGMAN
Worked with MAX VON SYDOW on:
The Seventh Seal (1956), *Wild Strawberries* (1957), *Virgin Spring* (1960), *Through A Glass Darkly* (1961), *Winter Light* (1962), *The Shame* (1968), *The Touch* (1971)

D

5 DIRECTORIAL DEBUTS NOMINATED FOR OSCARS

Orson Welles (*Citizen Kane*, 1941)
Sidney Lumet (*Twelve Angry Men*, 1957)
Mike Nichols (*Who's Afraid of Virginia Woolf?*, 1966)
Robert Redford (*Ordinary People*, 1980)
Kevin Costner (*Dances with Wolves*, 1990)

35 STARS WHO DIRECTED THEMSELVES IN FILMS

Buster Keaton (*The General*, 1927)
Charlie Chaplin (*The Great Dictator*, 1940)
Robert Montgomery (*Lady in the Lake*, 1946)
Laurence Olivier (*Hamlet*, 1948)
Ida Lupino (*The Bigamist*, 1953)
Burt Lancaster (*The Kentuckian*, 1955)
John Wayne (*The Alamo*, 1960)
Marlon Brando (*One-Eyed Jacks*, 1961)
Frank Sinatra (*None But the Brave*, 1965)
Albert Finney (*Charlie Bubbles*, 1968)
Richard Burton (*Dr. Faustus*, 1968)
Dennis Hopper (*The Last Movie*, 1971)
Charlton Heston (*Antony and Cleopatra*, 1973)
Sidney Poitier (*Uptown Saturday Night*, 1974)
Gene Wilder (*The World's Greatest Lover*, 1977)
Jack Nicholson (*Goin' South*, 1978)
James Caan (*Hide in Plain Sight*, 1979)
Alan Alda (*The Four Seasons*, 1981)

D

Burt Reynolds (*Sharky's Machine*, 1981)

Barbra Streisand (*Yentl*, 1983)

Anthony Perkins (*Psycho 3*, 1986)

Emilio Estevez (*Wisdom*, 1987)

Eddie Murphy (*Harlem Nights*, 1989)

Dan Aykroyd (*Nothing But Trouble*, 1991)

Jodie Foster (*Little Man Tate*, 1991)

Clint Eastwood (*Unforgiven*, 1992)

Billy Crystal (*Mr. Saturday Night*, 1992)

Danny de Vito (*Hoffa*, 1992)

Gary Sinise (*Of Mice and Men*, 1992)

Tim Robbins (*Bob Roberts*, 1992)

Robert de Niro (*A Bronx Tale*, 1993)

Mel Gibson (*The Man Without a Face*, 1993)

Ed Burns (*The Brothers McMullen*, 1995)

Albert Brooks (*Mother*, 1996)

Robert Redford (*The Horse Whisperer*, 1998)

5 DIRECTORS BEING UNASHAMEDLY CRUEL

ALFRED HITCHCOCK
In order to achieve authenticity during the making of *The Birds* (1963), he attached a number of sea gulls to Tippi Hedren's clothing and watched them struggle free. One of them nearly gouged her eye out in its panic to get away.

VICTOR FLEMING
Couldn't get Lana Turner to cry on cue for a scene in *Dr. Jekyll and Mr. Hyde* (1941), so in a fit of rage he grabbed her arm and twisted it sharply behind her back until the waterworks started.

ORSON WELLES

For Joseph Cotton's drunk scene in *Citizen Kane* (1941), Welles made him stay up all night to achieve the effect he wanted.

FRANCIS FORD COPPOLA

To make Claire Danes shudder for a scene in *The Rainmaker* (1997) in which she'd just been beaten by her husband, Coppola shoved ice cubes down her back.

JOHN FORD

To get Victor McLaglen suitably incensed for his famous fight scene with John Wayne in *The Quiet Man* (1952), Ford told him his performance in the movie thus far was substandard. McLaglen came out the next morning like a thing possessed and proceeded to beat the lard out of the Duke.

5 DIRECTORS BEING PERSNICKETY

MERVYN LEROY

This committed director of *Little Caesar* (1930) actually taped Edward G. Robinson's eyelids open for the final scene of the movie in order to give him a reptilian look.

WILLIAM WYLER

For the famous chariot scene in *Ben Hur* (1959), he assembled 8,000 extras, spending three months shooting what amounted to a twenty-minute sequence.

RICHARD ATTENBOROUGH

For the funeral scene in *Gandhi* (1982), the director painstakingly shot 20,000 feet of film, which was longer than the actual film itself. He employed eleven camera crews and 300,000 extras, but the final sequence was edited down to two minutes.

ALFRED HITCHCOCK

The famous shower scene in *Psycho* (1960) was achieved by a montage of seventy-eight separate shots spliced together into a deftly edited forty-five seconds of unforgettable terror.

HUMPHREY BOGART

Directed John Huston in a few of the scenes in which Huston himself was appearing in *The Treasure of the Sierra Madre* (1948). Bogart had great fun making Huston repeatedly redo the few scenes entrusted to him.

15 ACTORS WHO BECAME DIRECTORS BUT DIDN'T APPEAR IN THEIR FILMS

Leonard Nimoy (*Three Men and a Baby*, 1987)

Charles Laughton (*The Night of the Hunter*, 1955)

Paul Newman (*Rachel Rachel*, 1968)

Sean Penn (*The Crossing Guard*, 1995)

Anthony Quinn (*The Buccaneer*, 1958)

Robert Redford (*Ordinary People*, 1980)

Richard Benjamin (*Mermaids*, 1991)

Mel Gibson (*The Passion of the Christ*, 2004)

Jack Lemmon (*Kotch*, 1971)

Forrest Whitaker (*Hope Floats*, 1998)

Arnold Schwarzenneger (*Christmas in Connecticut*, 1992)

Robert Duvall (*Angelo, My Love*, 1983)

Dennis Hopper (*Colors*, 1988)

Sidney Poitier (*Stir Crazy*, 1981)

Warren Beatty (*Reds*, 1981)

HUSBANDS AND WIVES
15 men who've directed their wives

Neil Jordan: Beverly D'Angelo (*The Miracle*, 1991)
Nicolas Roeg: Theresa Russell (*Bad Timing*, 1980)
Sean Penn: Robin Wright (*The Crossing Guard*, 1995)
Brian de Palma: Nancy Allen (*Dressed to Kill*, 1980)
Charlie Chaplin: Paulette Godard (*Modern Times*, 1936)
Orson Welles: Rita Hayworth (*The Lady from Shanghai*, 1948)
Vincente Minnelli: Judy Garland (*The Pirate*, 1948)
Renny Harlin: Geena Davis (*Cutthroat Island*, 1995)
Warren Beatty: Annette Bening (*Bugsy*, 1991)
Blake Edwards: Julie Andrews (*That's Life*, 1986)
Kenneth Branagh: Emma Thompson (*Much Ado About Nothing*, 1993)
Roberto Rossellini: Ingrid Bergman (*Voyage to Italy*, 1953)
Mel Brooks: Anne Bancroft (*To Be Or Not To Be*, 1983)
Paul Newman: Joanne Woodward (*Rachel, Rachel*, 1968)
John Derek: Bo Derek (*Bolero*, 1984)

A STAR IS BORN
How 10 actors were discovered

JOHN WAYNE
By Raoul Walsh one day in 1928, when Wayne was loading furniture from a warehouse onto a truck.

GEORGE RAFT
Was sent to Texas Guinan's nightclub to extract protection money from her and she made him an offer that he couldn't refuse.

D

CLARK GABLE
Was repairing the phone of a drama coach fourteen years his senior…and ended up marrying her.

RYAN O'NEAL
At a gym by actor Richard Egan.

ROCK HUDSON
While working as a truck driver for the Budget Pack Company in 1954.

ANDY DEVINE
Walking down Sunset Boulevard one day in a football sweater… because a director standing nearby wanted somebody to play an athlete in a studio serial.

HARRISON FORD
By George Lucas on the set of *Star Wars* (1977), not realizing he was there to do carpentry work rather than to audition for a role.

WALTER BRENNAN
After doing a voice-over for a director who was having difficulty getting a donkey to bray on cue.

JOHNNY WEISSMULLER
Found himself auditioning for the part of Tarzan because he wanted to meet Clark Gable and there was no other way he could get into the studio.

FATTY ARBUCKLE
Was unblocking Mack Sennett's drain when he was offered his first role in a Keystone Cops movie.

AND 5 ACTRESSES...

JANET LEIGH
Norma Shearer saw a photograph of her at a ski lodge in California.

LAUREN BACALL
Howard Hawks saw her portrait in a magazine and screen-tested her for *To Have and Have Not* (1945).

JUDY GARLAND
Offered an MGM contract by mistake when Sam Goldwyn confused her with Deanna Durbin.

LANA TURNER
While drinking a Coke in an ice-cream parlor across the street from a high school in 1936.

CAROLE LOMBARD
While playing baseball outside the home of some friends of director Alan Dwan.

GOREFESTS
15 disgusting scenes from movies

Indiana Jones and the Temple of Doom (1984)
A high priest prises the heart out of one his victims...while it's still beating.

Videodrome (1982)
James Woods' stomach cavity becomes a repository for, what else, videocassettes.

Crash (1998)
James Spader, Holly Hunter, and Rosanna Arquette get sick
kicks from different types of things that go bump in the night.
Like, would you believe, automobiles?

Reservoir Dogs (1991)
Get an earful of Michael Madson hacking a cop's face off to the
background vocals of "Super Sounds of the 1970s".

Pink Flamingos (1974)
One of the characters eats doggie-doo and then blows a kiss.

The Shining (1980)
Rotting corpses in the bathtub, rivers of blood running through
eerie corridors, and Jack Nicholson coming up with a novel cure
for writer's block: i.e. an ax.

Seven (1996)
Kevin Spacey forces a very fat man to gorge himself to death on
food.

Face/Off (1998)
John Travolta steals Nicolas Cage's visage and then Nic has the
barefaced cheek to take Travolta's.

The Hitcher (1986)
Just when you thought it was safe to go back into the restaurant
… C. Thomas Howell is surveying his plate of French fries when
he spots, you've guessed it, a finger in its midst. An original
variation on the shaggy old fly-in-my-soup formula.

A Clockwork Orange (1971)
Malcolm McDowell trills "Singin' in the Rain" as he rapes Patrick Magee's wife.

There's Something About Mary (1998)
Matt Dillon tries to revive a doped dog by giving him home-made electric shock treatment courtesy of two lampshade cords.

Mimic (1998)
Mira Sorvino wipes bug goo all over her face in an attempt to persuade rampaging insects that she's one of them.

Cape Fear (1991)
Robert de Niro's hickey to his enthusiastic bed partner is a bit, how d'you say, extreme? In fact, he rips half her face off.

The Abyss (1989)
James Cameron submerges a rat in oxygenated fluid in this pre-*Titanic* underwater caper. Not exactly the stuff of Mary Poppins.

Bad Lieutenant (1992)
Harvey Keitel stops two pretty girls for a minor traffic violation and threatens to take them "downtown" unless they accede to his wishes. He tells one of them to take her skirt off so he can see her ass and makes the other perform the not-inconsiderable feat of miming oral sex. Meanwhile, he masturbates in front of the automobile.

LOOK HOMEWARD, ANGEL
10 domestic curiosities

PERRY COMO
The seventh son of a seventh son.

MONTGOMERY CLIFT
Had a twin sister.

LON CHANEY
Both of his parents were deaf mutes.

MARLON BRANDO
Both of his parents were alcoholics.

RED SKELTON
The son of a circus clown.

RUDOLPH VALENTINO
After he died, his brother was recruited to try and fill his shoes;
a plastic surgeon even worked on his nose to make him resemble
Rudolph more.

ROD CAMERON
Married his own mother-in-law.

CHER
Her mother was married eight times.

JACK NICHOLSON
Grew up believing that his sister was his mother.

CHARLES BRONSON
One of fifteen children, he says that the only childhood contact
he had with his mother was when she took him between her
knees to pull lice out of his hair.

DEDICATED FOLLOWERS OF FASHION

15 weird tales of the stars' dress sense

JOAN COLLINS

Wore a dress to a press conference in 1982 made from all the newspaper stories that were written about her that year.

KIM BASINGER

Says she loves garters so much that she even wears them *outside* her clothing.

YUL BRYNNER

Clad himself totally in black for the last four decades of his life, claiming that it made shopping easier.

DAVID LYNCH

Likes to keep one of his shoelaces untied.

JOHN RITTER

Wore his pyjamas onto a movie set in 1977 in protest at having to work on his honeymoon.

KIRK DOUGLAS

Used to change into his pyjamas as a "gentle" hint to guests who stayed too late at his parties that it was time to go home.

ROBERT MITCHUM

His wardrobe for *The Big Sleep* (1978), he said, consisted of a suit that had previously been worn by Victor Mature and Michael Caine "and not cleaned since."

MAE WEST

Wore ten-inch heels. And false nipples.

JOHN WAYNE
Wore lifts inside his shoes and a corset.

CHARLES BRONSON
Used to wear his sisters' hand-me-down dresses as a child, as his parents couldn't afford to buy him clothes of his own.

GEORGE HAMILTON
Throws away pairs of socks after wearing them just once.

CLARK GABLE
When he appeared wearing no undershirt in *It Happened One Night* (1934), sales of undershirts around the world plummeted.

IDA LUPINO
The gown she wore in *The Man I Love* (1946) was so tight that she passed out on the set. It eventually had to be cut off her before she was resuscitated.

CLINT EASTWOOD
Wore the same poncho for all three of his spaghetti westerns – without washing it.

LANA TURNER
Once owned 698 pairs of shoes.

IN VINO VERITAS
10 stars on the demon drink

"What contemptible scoundrel stole the cork out of my breakfast?" W. C. Fields

"The trouble with the world is that everybody is three drinks behind." Humphrey Bogart

D

"I was T.T. until Prohibition." Groucho Marx

"I'd hate to be a teetotaler. Imagine getting up in the morning and knowing that's as good as you're going to feel all day."
Dean Martin

"Some years ago a couple of friends of mine stopped drinking suddenly and died in agony. I swore then that such a thing should never happen to me." John Barrymore

"My father considered that anyone who went to chapel and didn't drink alcohol was not to be tolerated. I grew up in that belief." Richard Burton

"Hell, I used to take two-week lunch hours." Spencer Tracy

"I try not to drink too much, because when I'm drunk I bite."
Bette Midler

"The reason I drink is because when I'm sober I think I'm Eddie Fisher." Dean Martin

"Straight tequila is a real polite drink. You keep drinking until it won't go down. At that stage, you know you've reached your limit." Lee Marvin

DAYS OF WINE AND ROSES
5 drinking quotes from the movies

"I only take a drop when I have a cold. Of course, that cold has been hanging on for years."
(Frank Morgan in *Summer Holiday*, 1948)

"I always start around noon, in case it gets dark early."
(Peggy Lee in *Pete Kelly's Blues*, 1955)

"I've had hangovers before, but this time even my hair hurts."
(Rock Hudson in *Pillow Talk*, 1959)

"Give me a glass of lemonade—in a dirty glass."
(Bob Hope doing his best to be virile in *The Road to Utopia*, 1945)

"My mouth is so dry they could shoot Lawrence of Arabia in it."
(Dyan Cannon in *The Last of Sheila*, 1973)

THE NEEDLE AND THE DAMAGE DONE
10 stars who had drug problems

ROBERT DOWNEY, JR.
His penchant for overdoing the cocaine/heroin thing has landed him behind bars.

CHARLIE SHEEN
A few violent experiences on coke saw him come close to losing not only his career but his life.

D

DREW BARRYMORE
Became an alcoholic and a junkie when she was hardly out of the cradle, but has now embraced an eco-friendly lifestyle.

JACK NICHOLSON
Has been snorting since the 1960s—sometimes even before the camera if we're to believe the stories about the famous campfire scene in *Easy Rider* (1969).

STACY KEACH
Tried to smuggle 31 grams of cocaine into America in 1984, which resulted in him spending nine months in the slammer.

ROBERT MITCHUM
Busted for smoking pot in the 1940s, which was rather a scandal at that time. He went easy on it after that, although he still managed to look stoned every time he stepped out in front of a camera.

CARRIE FISHER
Dragged herself back from the hallucinogenic precipice to become a born-again author (*Postcards from the Edge*).

ELVIS PRESLEY
Never seemed to realize that you can kill yourself just as easily with the prescribed stuff if you take enough.

RIVER PHOENIX
Paid the ultimate price for going the John Belushi road of ingesting cocaine/heroin speedballs, becoming yet another one of Tinseltown's tarnished Lancelots vomiting his innards into a gutter before being carted away in a body-bag.

DENNIS HOPPER
Claims that he was once so strung out on dope that he walked out onto the wing of a plane as it was about to take off.

CURTAIN CALLS
10 classic movie end-lines

"For a minute there, I thought we were in trouble."
Butch Cassidy and the Sundance Kid, 1969

"Louis, I think this is the beginning of a beautiful friendship."
Casablanca, 1942

"All right, Mr. De Mille, I'm ready for my close-ups now."
Sunset Boulevard, 1950

"Made it Ma, top o' the world!" *White Heat*, 1949

"Shut up and deal!" *The Apartment*, 1960

"Nobody's perfect." *Some Like It Hot*, 1959

"Tomorrow is another day." *Gone with the Wind*, 1939

"Come back, Shane!" *Shane*, 1953

"Listen, who do I have to fuck to get OFF this picture?"
Blue Movie, 1968

"Marry me, Emily, and I'll never look at another horse."
A Day at the Races, 1937

ALTERED STATES
10 different endings to films

Dr. Strangelove (1964)
Stanley Kubrick's original ending had Peter Sellers involved in a
pie-throwing escapade in the Pentagon as he trilled "For He's a
Jolly Good Fellow," but he decided that this would render the
mushroom-cloud scene that preceded it anticlimactic so he
(wisely) left it out.

Invasion of the Body Snatchers (1956)
The first version of this slice of extraterrestrial kitsch had Kevin
McCarthy running through the streets frantically warning
innocent bystanders, "You're next!"

Double Indemnity (1944)
Fred MacMurray was executed by the State for his sins in Billy
Wilder's original print—as befitted killers of the Hays Code
era. Wilder then thought better of it and instead ended it with
McMurray being shot by Barbara Stanwyck as he attempts to
flee to Mexico.

A Farewell to Arms (1932)
In a burst of saccharine whimsy, Paramount dispensed with the
death of Catherine Barkley and, much to Ernest Hemingway's
dismay, let her live. (In the European version, however, she does
indeed die.)

Fatal Attraction (1987)
The original ending (still shown in Japan) had Glenn Close
topping herself in her grief, but American audiences preferred

the she-devil angle, much to Ms. Close's (righteous) indignation about the film's sexist overtones.

The Strange Affair of Uncle Harry (1945)

Robert Siodmak's *noir* thriller was saddled with an ending that transformed the whole thing into a dream. The censors of the 1940s could not allow George Sanders' character to get away with murder unchecked.

Five Easy Pieces (1970)

The original ending had Jack Nicholson dying in a crash, but he persuaded Bob Rafelson to shoot a much more downbeat (and more realistic) finale.

The Godless Girl (1929)

Cecil B. De Mille's story of an atheist who finally finds God was a big hit in Russia…after they had deleted the conversion.

Apocalypse Now (1979)

Francis Ford Coppola also shot a 35mm version where Willard, the Martin Sheen character, napalms the whole camp belonging to Kurtz after killing him.

Shane (1953)

In George Steven's first version, Shane ends up having sex with Marian on the tree stump, while Starrett goes into Grafton's to engage in the first homosexual encounter in a Western movie with Jack Wilson. (Only kidding.)

THE BIG PICTURE
the 10 most expensive movies ever made

Titanic ($200 million, 1998)
Waterworld ($175 million, 1995)
Dante's Peak ($116 million, 1997)
Star Wars: The Phantom Menace ($115 million, 1999)
Batman and Robin ($110 million, 1997)
Tomorrow Never Dies ($110 million, 1997)
True Lies ($110 million, 1994)
Speed 2 ($110 million, 1997)
Inchon ($102 million, 1981)
Batman Forever ($100 million, 1995)

UNDELETED
Hollywood expletives

CLARA BOW
Had it written into her contract with Paramount that no member of the film crew was allowed to use swear words within her earshot.

DAVID O. SELZNICK
Was fined $5,000 for allowing Clark Gable to say "Frankly, my dear, I don't give a damn" in *Gone with the Wind* (1939). The damage was mitigated when he put the emphasis on "give" instead of "damn."

RICHARD BURTON
Was the first actor to use the word "bugger" on screen in *Who's Afraid of Virginia Woolf?* (1966).

EDDIE MURPHY
Holds the record for the greatest number of swearwords in a movie: that's 262 in *Harlem Nights* (1989).

AL PACINO
He says "fuck" 183 times in *Scarface* (1983). Joan Collins quipped, "That's more than most people get in a lifetime."

A CAST OF THOUSANDS
10 films that used the most extras

Gandhi (300,000) 1982
Kolberg (187,000) 1945
Monster Wang-magwi (157,000) 1967
War and Peace (120,000) 1967
Ilya Muromets (106,000) 1956
Tonko (100,000) 1988
The War of Independence (80,000) 1912
Around the World in Eighty Days (69,000) 1956
Intolerance (60,000) 1916
Day Zrady (60,000) 1972

THAT LITTLE BIT EXTRA
10 stars who started out as extras

Merle Oberon	Stewart Granger
David Niven	Gary Cooper
Marilyn Monroe	Marlene Dietrich
Sophia Loren	Clark Gable
Jean Harlow	Rudolph Valentino

HOLLYWOOD OR BUST
15 ways to become famous without having talent

Nick Nolte: chew the scenery
Harrison Ford: look clumsy
Priscilla Presley: marry an icon
Kenneth Branagh: shout a lot in iambic pentameter
Clint Eastwood: whisper
Liz Hurley: wear revealing dresses
Hugh Grant: curb crawl
Nicolas Cage: ring Uncle Francis
Kim Basinger: pout
Alec Baldwin: marry Kim Basinger
Barbra Streisand: warble
Sharon Stone: flash
Goldie Hawn: giggle a lot
Roger Moore: act with your eyebrows
James Dean: die

HEAVEN'S GATE
10 famous last words

GEORGE SANDERS
"Dear World, I am leaving you because I am bored. I am leaving
you with your worries. Good luck." (Suicide note)

HUMPHREY BOGART
"I should never have switched from scotch to martinis."

BING CROSBY
"That was a great game of golf, fellas."

ERICH VON STROHEIM
"This isn't the worst. The worst is that Hollywood stole twenty-five years of my life."

JAMES DEAN
"That guy up there's gotta stop." (Just before his fatal car accident)

LOU COSTELLO (attributed)
"That was the best ice-cream soda I ever tasted."

W. C. FIELDS
"All in all I'd prefer to be in Philadelphia."

DOUGLAS FAIRBANKS
"I never felt better."

RUDOLPH VALENTINO
"Don't pull down the blinds; I feel fine."

JOHN BARRYMORE
"Tell me, Gene: is it true that you're the illegitimate son of Buffalo Bill?" (To his screenwriter friend Gene Fowler)

THE 'F' WORD
10 examples of the price of fame

RIN TIN TIN
Was receiving up to 2,000 letters a day from adoring fans at one point. Enjoyed popularity greater than many human stars of his time, including Charlie Chaplin and Valentino.

F

CHARLES LAUGHTON
Said the price of stardom was going to a restaurant and, instead of getting your soup, being confronted with yet another Bligh impersonation from the waiter.

CLIFF RICHARD
A fan once sent him a piece of chewing gum asking him to chew it and then return it to her. (Another fan posted herself to him as a package.)

JOAN COLLINS
Had to have her garbage shredded in 1987 after she discovered that a Beverly Hills garbage collector was selling it to fans.

MICKEY MOUSE
Received 800,000 fan letters in 1933, which put mere humans in the shade. (Shirley Temple came closest three years later, with 730,000.)

RUDOLPH VALENTINO
Over 100,000 mourners attended his funeral, most of them female. It took them three days to file past his grave.

ELVIS PRESLEY
Whenever he wanted to see a movie, he had to rent out the theater to avoid being pestered by fans.

ELIZABETH TAYLOR
These days, when people rush up to her, she says, it's not to ask for her autograph but to check out her wrinkles.

BURT REYNOLDS
A fan once sent him a piece of pubic hair wrapped in wax paper. "Her proposal," Reynolds moaned, "wasn't for marriage."

STEVEN SPIELBERG
In August 1997, a man who said he had a fantasy about raping Spielberg was arrested in his backyard, equipped with razor blades, handcuffs, and a stun gun.

MY FAVORITE YEAR

20 stars name the films that they enjoyed making most

Steve McQueen (*An Enemy of the People*, 1977)
Rock Hudson (*Giant*, 1956)
Charlie Chaplin (*The Gold Rush*, 1945)
Michael Caine (*The Man Who Would Be King*, 1975)
Frank Sinatra (*From Here to Eternity*, 1953)
Richard Harris (*The Field*, 1990)
James Cagney (*Yankee Doodle Dandy*, 1942)
Elvis Presley (*King Creole*, 1958)
Jessica Lange (*Blue Sky*, 1994)
Peter Sellers (*Being There*, 1979)
Shirley MacLaine (*The Apartment*, 1960)
Burt Reynolds (*Deliverance*, 1972)
Tony Curtis (*The Boston Strangler*, 1968)
Jack Nicholson (*Easy Rider*, 1969)
Richard Burton (*The Spy Who Came in from the Cold*, 1966)
Robert de Niro (*King of Comedy*, 1982)
Paul Newman (*The Outrage*, 1964)
Kirk Douglas (*Lonely Are the Brave*, 1962)
Marlon Brando (*Burn*, 1970)
Gene Hackman (*Scarecrow*, 1972)

F

THE AMERICAN FILM INSTITUTE'S
20 FAVORITE FILMS (as chosen in 1998)

Gone with the Wind (1939)
The Wizard of Oz (1939)
Citizen Kane (1941)
Casablanca (1942)
It's a Wonderful Life (1946)
All About Eve (1950)
Sunset Boulevard (1950)
Singin' in the Rain (1952)
The African Queen (1954)
On the Waterfront (1954)
The Bridge on the River Kwai (1957)
Some Like It Hot (1959)
Psycho (1960)
Lawrence of Arabia (1962)
The Graduate (1967)
The Godfather (1972)
Chinatown (1974)
One Flew Over the Cuckoo's Nest (1975)
Star Wars (1977)
Schindler's List (1993)

MOVIE MILESTONES
10 firsts in film

The first Hollywood film: D. W. Griffiths' *In Old California* (1910).

The first motion pictures in color were shown in London in 1909. They only showed two colors, however. (It wasn't until 1930 that Technicolor developed full color, which was first used in Walt Disney shorts.)

The first talkie was *The Jazz Singer* (1927), starring Al Jolson.

The first British talkie was Alfred Hitchcock's *Blackmail* (1929).

Walt Disney's first feature film, *Snow White and the Seven Dwarfs* (1937), required two million drawings and three years' work.

The first in-flight movie ever screened was the silent version of Sir Arthur Conan Doyle's *The Lost World* (1925).

The first Academy Awards ceremony was held in the Hollywood Roosevelt Hotel in May 1929.

Jaws (1975) was the first movie to top $100 million in ticket sales.

Greta Garbo's first screen line, "Gimme a visky with a ginger ale on the side—and don't be stinchy, baby," in *Anna Christie* (1930).

Earthquake (1974) was the first film released in Sensurround, a low-frequency sound process which gives off sensations similar to seismic tremors.

FIRST PAST THE CENSORS

10 watersheds in censorship

Men kissing
Manslaughter (1922)

Women kissing
Morocco (1930)

Female nudity
Ecstasy (1933)

French kiss
Splendour in the Grass (1961)

Male nudity
Zorba the Greek (1964)

Pubic hair
Blow-Up (1966)

Male organs
Women in Love (1970)

Bowel movement
Catch 22 (1970)

Irreverent animation
Fritz the Cat (1972)

Disney film to use the word "fuck"
Down and Out in Beverly Hills (1986)

DOWN AND OUT IN BEVERLY HILLS

the 10 greatest Hollywood flops of all time (estimated loss in brackets)

Cutthroat Island, 1995 ($81 million)
The Adventures of Baron Munchausen, 1989 ($48 million)
Ishtar, 1987 ($47 million)
Hudson Hawk, 1991 ($47 million)
1492: Conquest of Paradise, 1992 ($46 million)
The Cotton Club, 1984 ($38 million)
Santa Claus – The Movie, 1985 ($37 million)
Heaven's Gate, 1980 ($34 million)
Billy Bathgate, 1991 ($33 million)
Pirates, 1986 ($30 million)

THE LITTLE SHIPS THAT COULDN'T

10 stars reminiscing on their flops

"Cutting *Arch of Triumph* has improved it considerably. It was terrible for four hours, but now it is only terrible for two hours." (Charles Boyer)

"An exhibitor said *One from the Heart* was the worst film he'd seen in ten years. That's what the San Francisco exhibitors said about *Apocalypse Now* three years ago. So it

can only be the worst film he's seen in three years."
(Francis Ford Coppola)

"My biggest failure was *The Prodigal*. I liked the script. What I
forgot was that Cecil B. De Mille had an exclusive on the
Bible." (Dore Schary)

"I made a film called *Edge Of Doom*…and that's where it
brought all our careers." (Farley Granger)

"*Vendetta* wasn't released, it escaped!" (George Dolenz)

"*Moment by Moment*—that was the first time I heard the words,
'Your career is over.'" (John Travolta)

"*The Eddie Cantor Story*—if that's my life, I didn't live."
(Eddie Cantor)

"If you saw me in *The Adventures of Marco Polo*, you belong to
a very exclusive club." (Gary Cooper)

"I have two memories of *Saint Joan*. The first is being burned at
the stake in the picture, the second being burned by the critics.
The latter hurt more." (Jean Seberg)

"Jack Benny drove up to Warner Studios one night and said to
the guard at the gate, 'I made a movie here called *The Horn
Blows at Midnight*. Did you see it?' And the guard answered,
"See it? I directed it!'" (Milt Josefsberg)

FOOD, GLORIOUS FOOD
10 edible anecdotes

HOWARD HUGHES
For the last fifteen years of his life he lived almost entirely on ice cream.

ELVIS PRESLEY
A junk-food addict, he often gagged on his mixes of banana splits, cheeseburgers, and peanut butter sandwiches. Sometimes his bodyguards had to put their fingers down his throat to dislodge food caught in his windpipe. His favourite concoction was the 42,000-calorie Colorado sandwich, which comprised creamy peanut butter, grape jelly, and lean bacon fried to a crisp inside an entire loaf of bread that had been hollowed out and sliced lengthwise.

DAVID LYNCH
For seven years he ordered the same meal at a diner at 2:30 P.M. every afternoon.

FRANCIS FORD COPPOLA
To feed his cast members during the shooting of *Apocalypse Now* (1979), this director flew in fresh pasta every week from Italy to the Philippines at a cost of $8,000 a trip.

CLORIS LEACHMAN
Accidentally ate her own facial wart during the making of *Young Frankenstein* (1974), when it fell into a tuna sandwhich she was eating and disappeared into the mayonnaise.

NICK NOLTE
Ate real dog food for a scene in *Down and Out in Beverly Hills* (1986) when he was showing a dog how to use a food bowl.

JUDY GARLAND
During the making of *The Wizard of Oz* (1939), Twentieth Century Fox forced her to fast on alternate days so that she would more closely resemble the gaunt 11-year-old Dorothy.

GRETA GARBO
When Howard Dietz, not one of Garbo's favorite publicists, asked her once, "How would you like to come out for dinner on Monday?" she replied, "How do you know I'm going to be hungry on Monday?"

ALFRED HITCHCOCK
Once gave a dinner party where all the food was dyed blue.

JAMES CAGNEY
No restaurateur ever forgot him smashing a grapefruit into Mae Clark's face in *The Public Enemy* (1931), and he received offers of complimentary grapefruits off and on for the rest of his life. (To eat, that is.)

STAR WARS
15 cases of movie set–friction

BETTE DAVIS
Had a legendary feud with Joan Crawford, which reached its nadir when she said, "The best time I ever had with Joan in a film was when I pushed her down the stairs in *Whatever Happened to Baby Jane?*"

JAMES MASON
Said Raquel Welch was "the rudest, most unprofessional actress I've ever had the displeasure of working with. If I could, I'd spank her from here to Aswan."

SOPHIA LOREN
She didn't get on with Marlon Brando during the shooting of *The Countess from Hong Kong* (1966), especially after the day they were doing a love scene and he commented, "Did you know you have hairs up your nostrils?"

ANTHONY HOPKINS
Called Shirley MacLaine "the most obnoxious actress I've ever worked with" after appearing with her in *A Change of Seasons* (1980).

CHRISTOPHER PLUMMER
After making *The Sound of Music* (1965) with Julie Andrews, he said that working with her was "like being hit over the head with a Valentine card."

KRIS KRISTOFFERSON
After he made *A Star is Born* (1976) with Barbra Streisand, he commented: "Working with Barbra almost cured me of movies. It's like sitting down to a picnic in the middle of a freeway."

WILLIAM WYLER
His estimation of Frances Farmer was succinct: "The nicest thing I can say about Frances is that she's unbearable."

ALAN LADD
Compared the experience of working with Sophia Loren in *Boy on a Dolphin* (1957) to being "bombed by watermelons."

ROCK HUDSON
After working with Julie Andrews, he said, "There's nothing I wouldn't say to her face—both of them."

ORSON WELLES
Hated Peter Sellers so much that he insisted on shooting a scene they shared in the spy spoof *Casino Royale* (1967) on separate days. Both appeared at a gambling table together in the movie, but they were actually playing their lines to dummies.

MARLON BRANDO

During the famous "Brother Charlie" scene in *On the Waterfront* (1954), Brando left the set early, leaving costar Rod Steiger to deliver his lines to an empty wall. Steiger carried a grudge about this until 1997, when he made peace with his old rival.

FRANK SINATRA

Sinatra had bad vibes about Brando after being passed over for the *Waterfront* role. His animosity flared up during the making of *Guys and Dolls* (1955) with Brando the following year: during the restaurant scene, where Sinatra had to eat some cheesecake, and Brando insisted upon retake after retake (in contrast to "one-take-Frank"), Sinatra eventually exploded with the classic line: "Just how much fucking cheesecake can a man eat?"

CHARLIE SHEEN

Became so aggravated by Sean Young on the set of *Wall Street* (1987) that he pinned a note to her back with the words "I am a bitch" written on it.

TONY CURTIS

Had an affair with Marilyn Monroe during the making of *Some Like It Hot* (1959), but still managed to say that kissing her was like kissing Hitler. The comment was figurative: she drove him batty by being continually late on set and fluffing takes. Director Billy Wilder always used her best rather than Tony's, which didn't help, as he was hardly able to give it his best by take twenty-three, which was when Marilyn was just warming to her task.

KLAUS KINSKI

Had a gun pulled on him on the set of *Aguirre, Wrath of God* (1972) by the director Werner Herzog, after he'd threatened to leave the film. Herzog threatened to kill Kinski and then himself if he tried to walk away. In 1982, when the two were again working together on *Fitzcarraldo*, Herzog attempted to murder Kinski by setting fire to a house in which he slept.

G

OOPS!
20 movie blunders

The Invisible Man (1933)
His footprints are shown as the prints of shoes rather than bare feet in one scene. Obviously he didn't wear shoes or they would have been seen.

Presumed Innocent (1990)
When Harrison Ford is besieged by reporters, one of them thrusts an empty tape recorder into his face.

Cocktail (1988)
Tom Cruise passes a movie theater where *Barfly* is playing. A few minutes later, the same theater is showing *Casablanca*.

Rear Window (1954)
James Stewart's plaster cast moves from his left leg to his right for a whole scene.

Jagged Edge (1985)
Glenn Close goes into court wearing a drab gray suit. First it changes to a dark blue outfit with a white blouse, then it becomes a brown ensemble, and then it goes back to blue again, but with a polka-dot blouse.

Pretty Woman (1990)
In the restaurant scene with Julia Roberts, Richard Gere, and Ralph Bellamy, all three are served sorbet. First of all Bellamy's drink disappears, then Gere's does and Bellamy gets his back. Then Roberts' drink disappears and Gere's returns.

The Bridge on the River Kwai (1957)
The main actor is listed as "Alec Guiness." Maybe the story-boarder had too many glasses of it to notice the misspelling...

Bullitt (1968)
The car-chasing Steve McQueen loses three hubcaps...and then three more.

Jailhouse Rock (1957)
Elvis Presley's prison uniform changes from number 6239 to 6240.

Dial M for Murder (1954)
Before Grace Kelly stabs Anthony Dowson, you can actually see the pair of scissors she uses embedded in his back.

Days of Thunder (1990)
At one point Tom Cruise (playing a character named Cole) is greeted with, "Hi, Tom."

Breakfast at Tiffany's (1961)
When Audrey Hepburn crawls through the window of George Peppard's bedroom she's wearing no stockings. A few moments later, she is.

Anatomy of a Murder (1959)
Lee Remick appears in a café in a snow-white dress. When she leaves it, she's in pants.

Star Wars (1977)
Luke Skywalker (Mark Hamill) addresses Carrie Fisher by her real name rather than as Princess Leia at one point.

It Happened One Night (1934)
Clark Gable leaves his hotel at 2:30 A.M., drives around New York, writes a story for his newspaper, and returns to his room. The time is still 2:30 on the clock.

Psycho (1960)
Janet Leigh gulps twice after she's killed in the famous shower scene.

Diamonds Are Forever (1971)
Sean Connery drives his automobile through a narrow alley on its two right wheels and it emerges on its two left ones. A good trick, even by 007's standards.

The King and I (1956)
Yul Brynner's earring keeps shifting from ear to ear.

The Untouchables (1987)
A "dead" body moves from one end of a room to the other.

Casablanca (1942)
Ingrid Bergman tells Bogie that she wore a dress on her last day in Paris, but the flashbacks reveal that she was dressed in a suit.

FROM "I DO" TO "I'LL SUE"
10 actresses who had to pay galimony to their ex-husbands

Roseanne	Jane Fonda	Lana Turner
Kim Basinger	Goldie Hawn	Joan Lunden
Joan Collins	Jessica Lange	
Phyllis Diller	Jane Seymour	

LET'S HAVE SOME NEW CLICHES
15 classic sayings of Sam Goldwyn

"I can answer you in two words: im possible."

"What we want is a story that starts with an earthquake and works its way up to a climax."

"I'll give you a definite maybe."

"We've all passed a lot of water since then."

"It's more than magnificent—it's mediocre."

"I don't want any yes men around me. I want everybody to tell me the truth—even if it costs them their jobs."

"Why did you call your baby John? Every Tom, Dick and Harry is called John these days."

"Anybody who goes to see a psychiatrist ought to have his head examined."

"Tell me, how did you love the picture?"

"Let's bring it up to date with some snappy nineteenth-century dialogue."

"You ought to take the bull between the teeth."

"I read part of the book all the way through."

"If you can't give me your word of honor, will you give me your promise?"

"My wife's hands are so beautiful I had a bust made of them."

"Too caustic? To hell with the cost—we'll make the picture anyway."

GONE WITH THE WIND
15 bits of trivia

Over eighty-three hours of footage were originally shot.

The total cast, including extras, numbered 4,400.

There were 1,400 candidates for the part of Scarlett O'Hara, but only one for Rhett Butler.

The movie contained 1,475 animals, comprising 1,100 horses and various pigs, mules, oxen, dogs, and turkeys.

The fabric for the women's costumes used in the movie stretched for 35,000 yards.

Scarlett wore a total of forty-four costumes in the film, compared to Rhett's thirty-six and Melanie's twenty-one.
(Ashley Wilkes weighed in with a paltry eleven.)

There were more than 20,000 words of dialogue in it, and 685 scenes.

It took more than two years to shoot.

Buying the rights to Margaret Mitchell's novel cost $50,000.

Norma Shearer was originally chosen for the part of Scarlett, but she bowed out after receiving an avalanche of "fan" mail informing her that she would be wrong for it. Other unsuccessful wannabes were Katharine Hepburn, Claudette Colbert, Lana Turner, Bette Davis, Joan Crawford, Jean Harlow, and Carole Lombard.

Leigh earned a (then) astronomical $15,000 for the role.

It was shown in Russia for the first time in 1989.

MGM refused the rights to the film. Louis B. Mayer had been swayed by one of his producers, who told him that no Civil War movie ever made a nickel.

David O. Selznick had to employ four directors and fifteen screenwriters before he found what he was looking for.

The total cost of the film was $4 million, which in today's terms puts it in the *Titanic* (1998) league.

"FRANKLY, MY DEAR..."
5 other classic lines from that movie

"Great balls of fire! Don't bother me anymore, and don't call me sugar!" (Scarlett O'Hara)

"With enough courage, you can do without a reputation." (Rhett Butler)

"Marriage, fun? Fiddle-dee-dee! Fun for men you mean." (Scarlett)

"I can't wait all my life waiting to catch you between husbands." (Rhett)

"After all...tomorrow is another day." (Scarlett)

KEEP YOUR HAIR ON
10 hair-raising experiences

PETER USTINOV
Was told to grow a beard for his part in *Quo Vadis* (1951), but the director decided that it looked too artificial so he got him to wear a false one instead.

DAVID NIVEN
Sam Goldwyn asked him to dye his hair blond for a role rather than wear a wig. A review of the finished film went, "Niven ruins his performance by wearing an appalling wig."

CAROLE LOMBARD
Was alleged even to have bleached her pubic hair to make people believe she was a natural blonde.

FAYE DUNAWAY
Became infuriated with Roman Polanski during a scene in *Chinatown* (1974) when he plucked a hair from her head which was sticking out and disturbing a shot. She never forgave him.

LANA TURNER
Had her eyebrows shaved off for *The Adventures of Marco Polo* (1938) and they never grew back.

HOWARD HUGHES
Only visited a barber twice in the last decade of his life.

KEVIN COSTNER
Cut his hair into the crew-cut style of Steve McQueen when making *The Bodyguard* (1992), a movie that had been originally earmarked for McQueen and Diana Ross.

Telly Savalas

Became traumatised when George Stevens told him that he wanted to shave his head to play Pontius Pilate in *The Greatest Story Ever Told* (1965). When he told Stevens he was nervous about his children's reaction to this, Stevens canceled production of the film for a day (at a cost of $60,000) in order to allow Telly's children to witness the shaving at first hand and thus approve it.

Sean Connery

Warner Brothers paid $52,000 for the toupee he used in *Never Say Never Again* (1983).

Anthony Quinn

After shaving his head for *The Magus* (1968), he inserted a clause in his contract whereby he would receive a huge remuneration if his hair didn't grow back. Fortunately (or maybe unfortunately!), it did.

HEALTH, HYGIENE, AND THE STARS

George Hamilton

Is such a health fanatic that he has a private blood bank in his own house.

Bud Abbott

He was an epileptic, and, at the start of an attack onstage, his partner Lou Costello would punch him in the stomach to try to shock him out of it. Audiences imagined that it was all part of their act and laughed uproariously.

Peter Sellers

Suffered eight heart attacks within of two hours one night.

ZSA ZSA GABOR

Whenever she had a fever as a child, her grandmother would cure it by prescribing champagne for her.

JOHN WAYNE

He had a heart valve replaced with one from the heart of a pig in 1978. This caused him to quip, "Make sure I don't have a curly tail when they bring me out of surgery."

VIVIEN LEIGH

Hated kissing Clark Gable during the shooting of *Gone with the Wind* (1939) because of the foul odor emanating from his dentures.

HOWARD HUGHES

His fear of bacteria was so intense that he wouldn't allow visitors in his front door without a thorough examination. He refused to touch anything without first wrapping his hand in a Kleenex.

JOAN CRAWFORD

Had all the bathtubs in her house removed, as she felt that it was unsanitary to sit in one's own bathtub water.

BING CROSBY

Used to hand-wash all his shirts before sending them to hotel laundries as he was embarrassed about the staff seeing the dirt.

WALT DISNEY

Used to wash his hands up to thirty times an hour for hygiene purposes.

SPECIFIC HEIGHTS
10 vertically challenged stars

Dustin Hoffman: 4' 11"
Gloria Swanson: 4'11½"
Danny de Vito: 5' 0"
Mary Pickford: 5' 0"
Dudley Moore: 5' 2½"

Lana Turner: 5' 3"
Mickey Rooney: 5' 3"
Michael J. Fox: 5' 4"
Humphrey Bogart 5' 4"
Al Pacino: 5' 6"

GOODBYE, MR. CHIPS
10 high-school dropouts

Richard Boone
Humphrey Bogart
Geneviève Bujold
Frank Sinatra
Dean Martin

Al Pacino
Steve McQueen
Cher
Drew Barrymore
Sylvester Stallone

DIAL "C" FOR CAMEO
10 famous Hitchcock cameos from his own movies

Blackmail (1929)
Swats a little boy with a newspaper while riding on the subway.

The Lady Vanishes (1938)
Smoking a cigarette at Victoria Station.

Rebecca (1940)
Waiting outside a telephone booth which George Sanders is using.

Lifeboat (1944)
Appears in a newspaper ad for an obesity corset.

Strangers on a Train (1951)
Boarding a train carrying a double bass.

Rear Window (1954)
Winds up a clock in the screenwriter's apartment.

North by Northwest (1959)
Running for a bus, only for the doors to close in his face.

Psycho (1960)
Standing in the street wearing a cowboy hat.

The Birds (1963)
Walks past Tippi Hedren in the street with two dogs.

Torn Curtain (1966)
Nursing a baby (that wets itself) in a hotel lobby.

HOLLYWOOD BABBLE ON
20 cynics give their views

"In Hollywood, you judge people by the level at which they compromise." (Lionel Stander)

"A town that has to be seen to be disbelieved." (Walter Winchell)

"You can seduce a man's wife there, attack his daughter, and wipe your hands on his canary—but if you don't like his movie, you're dead." (Josef von Sternberg)

"No one ever went broke in Hollywood underestimating the intelligence of the public." (Elsa Maxwell)

"In Hollywood if a guy's wife looks like a new woman… she probably is." (Dean Martin)

"Strip the phony tinsel off Hollywood and you'll find the real tinsel underneath." (Oscar Levant)

"It's not true that I was born a monster. Hollywood made me one." (Boris Karloff)

"Hollywood is a strange place if you're in trouble. Everybody thinks it's contagious." (Judy Garland)

"They've great respect for the dead in Hollywood, but none for the living." (Errol Flynn)

"In 1940 I had a choice between Hitler and Hollywood, but I preferred Hollywood. Just a little." (Rene Clair)

"I've had several years in Hollywood and I still think the real movie heroes are the people in the audience." (Walter Winchell)

"You can take all the sincerity in Hollywood, place it in the navel of a fruit fly, and still have room enough for three caraway seeds and a producer's heart." (Fred Allen)

"What I like about it is that one can get along fine by knowing just two words of English: swell and lousy." (Vicki Baum)

"I look upon going to Hollywood as a mission behind enemy lines. You parachute in, set up the explosion, then fly out before it goes off." (Robert Redford)

"When I'm 60, Hollywood will forgive me. I don't know for what, but it'll forgive me." (Steven Spielberg)

"If you stay in Beverly Hills too long, you become a Mercedes." (Dustin Hoffman)

"I don't spend too much time in Hollywood. I'm afraid I might wind up as one of Hugh Hefner's bunnies." (Liv Ullmann)

"Hollywood stinks." (Frank Sinatra)

"Until you're known in my profession as a monster, you're not a star." (Bette Davis)

"It's said in Hollywood that you should always forgive your enemies —because you never know when you'll have to work with them." (Lana Turner)

IDEAL HOLMES EXHIBITIONS
20 actors who portrayed Sherlock Holmes

Clive Brook (*The Return of Sherlock Holmes*, 1929)

Arthur Wortner (*The Sleeping Cardinal*, 1931)

Raymond Massey (*The Speckled Band*, 1931)

Robert Rendel (*The Hound of the Baskervilles*, 1932)

Martin Fric (*Lelicek in the Service of Sherlock Holmes*, 1932)

Reginald Owen (*A Study in Scarlet*, 1933)

Bruno Guttner (*Der Hund von Baskerville*, 1937)

Hermann Speelmans (*The Grey Lady*, 1937)

Hans Albers (*The Man Who Was Sherlock Holmes*, 1937)

Basil Rathbone (*The Hound of the Baskervilles*, 1939)

John Longden (*The Man with the Twisted Lip*, 1951)

Peter Cushing (*The Hound of the Baskervilles*, 1959)

Christopher Lee (*Sherlock Holmes and the Deadly Necklace*, 1962)

John Neville (*A Study in Terror*, 1965)

Robert Stephens (*The Private Life of Sherlock Holmes*, 1970)

Radovan Lukavsky (*Sherlock Holmes' Desire*, 1971)

Douglas Wilmer (*The Adventures of Sherlock Holmes' Smarter Brother*, 1975)

Nicol Williamson (*The Seven Per Cent Solution*, 1976)

Peter Cook (*The Hound of the Baskervilles*, 1978)

Christopher Plummer (*Murder by Decree*, 1979)

CAUSE CELEBS
10 Hollywood humanitarians

MARLON BRANDO
Refused an Oscar for *The Godfather* (1973) because of
Hollywood's brutal treatment of the American Indian.

JANE FONDA
Unkindly referred to as "Jane of Arc" when she was accused of
having a Messianic complex during the "Hanoi Jane" days.

VANESSA REDGRAVE
Fonda's friend, and a woman who has stood up for everything
from the PLO to the IRA to the Worker's Revolutionary Party.
Has received many death threats in the process.

RICHARD GERE
A Buddhist and good friend of the Dalai Lama, Gere has
protested against China's savage treatment of Tibetan people.

AUDREY HEPBURN
The sometime clotheshorse traded in her champagne-and-caviar
lifestyle for a pair of jeans and a few T-shirts when she went on
the road for UNICEF to war-ravaged countries like Somalia in
the last few years of her life.

PAUL NEWMAN
Has turned a casual hobby—the making of homemade oil-and-
vinegar salad dressing—into a multimillion-dollar business to
fund his famous Hole-in-the-Wall Gang camps which give annual vacations to children suffering from life-threatening diseases.

ELIZABETH TAYLOR
Hollywood's most devoted AIDS campaigner. She set up the
American Foundation for AIDS research.

Brigitte Bardot
Made the dubious transition from Women's Lib to Saving the Seal (and various other animals) when she said adieu to Hollywood in the early 1970s.

Christopher Reeve
Has become a vociferous spokesman (and fund-raiser) for the American Paralysis Association after a horrific riding accident in 1995 turned the former *Superman* star into a quadriplegic.

Frank Sinatra
Ol' Blue Eyes did it His Way even after the final curtain fell, leaving a fortune to charities supporting abused children.

TRUE CONFESSIONS
5 stars with a sense of humor about themselves

Veronica Lake
"You could put all the talent I had into your left eye and still not suffer from impaired vision."

Richard Burton
"I've done the most unutterable rubbish merely to have somewhere to go in the mornings."

Glenda Jackson
"I had no real ambition about acting, but I knew there had to be something better than the bloody chemist's shop."

Roger Moore
"My acting range? Left eyebrow raised, right eyebrow raised."

Bette Midler
"I wouldn't say I invented tack, but I definitely brought it to its present high popularity."

MOVE OVER, DARLING

25 husbands and wives who acted together

Liam Neeson and Natasha Richardson (*Nell*, 1994)

Bruce Willis and Demi Moore (*Mortal Thoughts*, 1991)

Michael and Shakira Caine (*The Man Who Would Be King*, 1975)

Paul Newman and Joanne Woodward (*Mr. and Mrs. Bridge*, 1990)

Humphrey Bogart and Lauren Bacall (*Key Largo*, 1948)

Richard Burton and Elizabeth Taylor (*Boom*, 1968)

Charlie Chaplin and Paulette Godard (*The Great Dictator*, 1940)

Charles Bronson and Jill Ireland (*The Mechanic*, 1972)

Sean Penn and Madonna (*Shanghai Surprise*, 1986)

Robert de Niro and Diahnne Abbot (*King of Comedy*, 1982)

Mary Pickford and Douglas Fairbanks (*The Taming of the Shrew*, 1967)

Tony Curtis and Janet Leigh (*The Black Shield of Falworth*, 1954)

Antonio Banderas and Melanie Griffith (*Too Much*, 1996)

Brooks West and Eve Arden (*Anatomy of a Murder*, 1959)

Ethan Hawke and Uma Thurman (*Gattaca*, 1998)

Sean Penn and Robin Wright (*She's So Lovely*, 1998)

Meg Ryan and Dennis Quaid (*D.O.A.*, 1988)

Harvey Keitel and Lorraine Bracco (*The Naples Connection*, 1985)

Tom Cruise and Nicole Kidman (*Eyes Wide Shut*, 1999)

Bruce Dern and Diane Ladd (*The Wild Angels*, 1966)

Tim Robbins and Susan Sarandon (*Bob Roberts*, 1992)

Gabriel Byrne and Ellen Barkin (*Into the West*, 1993)

Rachel Ward and Bryan Brown (*The Good Wife*, 1986)

Jeff Goldblum and Geena Davis (*Earth Girls Are Easy*, 1989)

Val Kilmer and Joanne Whalley-Kilmer (*Kill Me Again*, 1990)

THE FACE BEHIND THE MASK
10 stars talk about their identity

"I was more nervous presenting the Oscar ceremonies in 1984 than in any film role because I had no character to hide behind." (Mel Gibson)

"I'm not really Henry Fonda. Nobody could have that much integrity." (Henry Fonda)

"Every man I knew went to bed with Gilda…and woke up with me." (Rita Hayworth)

"If you asked me to play myself I wouldn't know what to do. I do not know who or what I am. There used to be a me, but I had it surgically removed." (Peter Sellers)

"The public has always expected me to be a playboy, and a decent chap never lets his public down." (Errol Flynn)

"When I'm involved in pub brawls, I'm called an Irishman, but when I win an acting awards I'm a Brit through and through." (Richard Harris)

"This king stuff is pure bull. I eat and drink and go to the bathroom just like everyone else. I'm just a lucky slob from Ohio who happened to be in the right place at the right time." (Clark Gable)

"I never go out unless I look like Joan Crawford the movie star. If you want to see the girl next door, go next door."
(Joan Crawford)

"My father cried when he saw me bleeding in films, but never when I shed real blood as a child." (Kirk Douglas)

"How can I fail, when I've got Brando on one side of me saying 'Fuck you', and Monty on the other saying, 'Help me.'"
(James Dean used to sign his letters 'James Brando-Clift Dean')

INDIAN IN THE CUPBOARD
5 stars with Native American blood

Cher
Roy Rogers
Burt Reynolds
James Garner
Johnny Depp

5 INITIALS AND WHAT THEY STAND FOR

Cecil B. De Mille (Blount)
W. C. Fields (William Claude)
George S. Kaufman (Simon)
D. W. Griffith (David Wark)
David O. Selznick (Oliver)

THE BEST POLICY
5 insurance oddities

JOHN HUSTON
Was uninsurable during his swansong movie *The Dead* (1988) because of his long and varied history of health problems.

CYD CHARISSE
Had her legs insured for a whopping $5 million. This was in the 1950s, so you could probably multiply that figure five times over to translate it into today's terms.

WALTER HEIRS
This character actor felt that his weight was so much a part of his appeal that he took out a $25,000 insurance premium against losing any.

JIMMY DURANTE
Similarly, Durante felt that his oversized nose was an integral part of his earning power, so he had it insured for $100,000.

COURTNEY LOVE
Was almost uninsurable for *The People vs. Larry Flynt* (1996) because of her heroin history, but she won the moguls over after promising to take weekly tests to prove that she was clean.

STIR CRAZY
15 actors who went to jail

RORY CALHOUN
Served three years for car theft.

ROBERT MITCHUM
Spent sixty days in jail in 1949 for possession of marijuana. After-ward, he claimed that it was the finest vacation he'd had in years. Was also sentenced to a chain gang for vagrancy in 1933.

TOMMY RETTIG
This child star of the 1950s (he appeared with Marilyn Monroe and Robert Mitchum in *River of No Return*, 1954) was sentenced to 5½ years in prison in 1976 for trying to smuggle cocaine into the USA from Peru.

FATTY ARBUCKLE
Arrested for allegedly killing a woman at a party in his house in 1921. He was finally acquitted after three trials, but his career was dead.

STACY KEACH
Did nine months in Reading Jail for trying to smuggle $8,000 worth of cocaine into Heathrow in a can of shaving cream.

STEVE MCQUEEN
Spent two years at reform school, and also twenty-one days for going AWOL from the navy.

GEORGE C. SCOTT
Put behind bars for a night after being drunk and disorderly.

BURT REYNOLDS
Sentenced to a week on a chain gang for vagrancy.

GRIFFIN O'NEAL
Was put behind bars for riddling his girlfriend's car with bullets from a .44 Magnum, Dirty Harry style.

TOM NEAL
In 1965 this leading star of the 1940s was jailed for seven years on a manslaughter charge after he shot his second wife Gail Kloke to death. The original charge was first-degree murder, but he said that it was an accident and the jury believed him. It was a mysterious case, as the gun was never found. Neal died of heart failure a few months after his release.

RICHARD PRYOR
Did ten days once for failing to make out his income tax return.

RUDOLPH VALENTINO
Jailed for three days in 1916 when vice squad detectives picked him up in a New York bordello on suspicion of being a gigolo, then again three years later for bigamy when he married Natacha Rambova before the annulment of his (one-day) marriage to Jane Acker came through.

AL PACINO
At the beginning of his career he did three days in jail, for possession of a concealed weapon.

CHRISTIAN SLATER
Jailed for nine months in 1997 after punching his girlfriend, biting a man in the stomach, and then assaulting the policeman who tried to arrest him. (After Slater subsequently threatened the police officer with his own gun, he was put in a chokehold until he passed out.)

CHARLIE SHEEN
Had a one-year suspended sentence imposed on him for battering an ex-lover after a coke binge. She received twenty-seven stitches to her lip after he smashed her head onto the floor and threatened to kill her.

5 ACTRESSES WHO DID TIME

MAE WEST
Jailed for ten days in 1927 for alleged indecent behavior during
the Broadway run of her play *Sex*. According to West, "The
police investigating me seemed to enjoy it."

SOPHIA LOREN
Spent a month in the clink in 1982 for tax evasion, which her
accountant euphemistically referred to as "a little error."

ZSA ZSA GABOR
Sentenced to three days in jail for slapping a traffic cop in 1989
after he allegedly dragged her out of a car and called her a
whore. (The officer subsequently sued her for defamation of
character, which cost her $100,000 in a lawsuit.)

FRANCES FARMER
Jailed in 1942 for resisting arrest after a drunk-driving violation.
At her court case she said to the judge, "Listen, I put liquor in
my milk, liquor in my coffee, and liquor in my orange juice.
What do you want me to do, starve to death?" She then threw an
inkwell at him, which resulted in her being carted out of the
courtroom in a straitjacket.

CLAUDINE LONGET
Andy Williams' ex served only thirty days in the slammer after
shooting her second husand, Vladimir Sabich. The jury bought
her story that the gun went off when he was showing her how to
use it.

JESUS CHRIST SUPERSTAR
15 stars who've portrayed the son of God

Golgotha (Robert Le Vigan 1935)
The Day of Triumph (Robert Wilson, 1954)
Ben Hur (Claude Heater, 1959)
King of Kings (Jeffrey Hunter, 1961)
Pontio Pilato (John Barrymore, 1961)
Barabbas (Roy Mangano, 1962)
The Gospel According to St. Matthew (Enrique Irazoqui 1964)
The Milky Way (Bernard Verley, 1969)
Jesus of Nazareth (Robert Powell, 1977)
Jesus (Brian Deacon, 1979)
The Day Christ Died (Chris Sarandon, 1980)
In Search of Historic Jesus (John Rubinstein, 1980)
History of the World Part 1 (John Hurt, 1981)
The Passion of the Christ (Jim Cavaziel, 2004)
The Last Temptation of Christ (Willem Dafoe, 1988)

NEVER GIVE A SUCKER A BREAK
10 stars who lost their jobs

DUSTIN HOFFMAN
Sacked from Ridley's restaurant as a young man for devouring
six steaks in succession from the restaurant's kitchen.

MADONNA
Fired from Dunkin' Donuts for squirting jam at a customer.

KENNETH MORE
Given his walking papers from Sainsbury's butter and egg counter because he broke so many eggs.

ROBERT REDFORD
Sacked from a construction site for losing his toolbox.

ERROL FLYNN
Dismissed from a position as police patrol officer in New Guinea when it was discovered he had been found rifling through the pettycash box in a previous job.

DANNY KAYE
Sacked from an insurance job after giving a client a check for $40,000 instead of $4,000.

JERRY LEWIS
Let go from a soda-fountain job after serving a banana split with the peel still on the banana. He had been in the job a whole hour before this oversight.

ROBERT MITCHUM
Sacked from a car factory in Toledo because he refused to wear socks to work.

PETER FINCH
Fired from a journalistic post after spilling a pitcher of water over an
editor's head.

ELVIS PRESLEY
Sacked from his job as a movie theater usher in the early 1950s when it transpired that one of the other employees was giving him free candy.

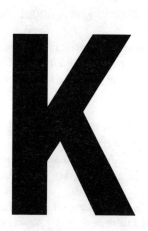

LIP-O-SUCTION
10 things you should know about movie kisses

The first kiss recorded on film in a motion picture was in Thomas Edison's *The Kiss* (1896). It took place between John Rice and May Irwin and played to nickelodeon audiences. It lasted for thirty seconds.

The movie with the most kisses is Warner Brothers' *Don Juan* (1926), starring John Barrymore. In the course of the 167-minute film, he bestows a total of 191 kisses on a number of beautiful senoritas—an average of one every fifty-three seconds.

The longest kiss in film history is between Jane Wyman and Regis Toomey in *You're in the Army Now* (1941). It lasts for three minutes and five seconds.

The most famous homosexual kiss in movies is that between Peter Finch and Murray Head in John Schlesinger's *Sunday Bloody Sunday* (1971).

Mae West never kissed a man on screen.

Marlene Dietrich's makeup man said she kissed so hard, she needed a new mouth after every kiss.

"I'm fond of kissing," Carrie Fisher told *Playboy* in 1983. "God sent me down to earth to kiss a lot of people."

Kim Basinger believes that there's an art to it: "You have to believe it's as good as what's coming later."

"Harrison Ford is so famous," Carrie Fisher said once, "he doesn't kiss with his own tongue any more—he uses someone else's."

Michael Caine had to kiss Christopher Reeve in a homosexual encounter in *Deathtrap* (1982), so they shared a bottle of brandy to work up the courage for the smooch.

TO SIR WITH LOVE...
10 actors or directors who've been knighted

Ralph Richardson
Laurence Olivier
Richard Attenborough
Michael Redgrave
David Lean
Ian McKellen
Anthony Hopkins
Noel Coward
John Gielgud
Alec Guinness

BE SUING YOU

5 stars who ended up in the law courts

JAMES WOODS
Filed a $6 million lawsuit against Sean Young in 1988. He claimed that his former costar left a doll on his doorstep covered in fake blood as a revenge gesture for the fact that he broke off their affair (conducted during the filming of *The Boost* the same year) to go back to his wife.

KIM BASINGER
Asked to pay almost $9 million to the makers of *Boxing Helena* (1993) after she dropped out of that film, having verbally contracted to appear in it. (Her costs were subsequently reduced.)

PAMELA ANDERSON
Sued by the makers of *Hello, She Lied* because she pulled out of the picture shortly before it was due to be shot. The reason she gave was that she was uncomfortable with nude scenes following a bad experience on a previous movie, *Ship Tracer*, but they alleged the real reason was because she wanted to make herself available for the bigger-budget *Barb Wire* (1996)—not a movie one could easily call chaste.

DOUGLAS FAIRBANKS
Sued for $500 after he accidentally plunged an arrow into the bottom of a tailor when doing a promo "shot" for *Robin Hood* (1922).

THE MARX BROTHERS
When Warner Brothers threatened to sue the anarchic siblings for their film title *A Night in Casablanca* (1946), which they said traded on their own *Casablanca*, Groucho told them that if they did he'd sue them for using the word "Brothers."

SOUTHPAWS
10 left-handed actors

Robert de Niro

W. C. Fields

Rock Hudson

Charlie Chaplin

Robert Redford

Tom Cruise

Rex Harrison

Danny Kaye

Harpo Marx

Terence Stamp

10 LEFT-HANDED ACTRESSES

Kim Novak

Betty Grable

Diane Keaton

Shirley MacLaine

Judy Garland

Julia Roberts

Marilyn Monroe

Goldie Hawn

Joanne Woodward

Olivia de Havilland

BASIC INSTINCTS
5 stars with star-sized libidos

GEORGE RAFT

Had a voracious appetite for sex, once making love to seven chorus girls in a single night. His usual daily average, however, was a mere two women.

ERROL FLYNN

Claimed that he spent between 12,000 and 14,000 nights of his life making love. (He put cocaine on his penis as an aphrodisiac.)

TALLULAH BANKHEAD

When asked why she was going to Hollywood after a successful theatrical career, she replied, "First for the money, second to make movies, and lastly to fuck that divine Gary Cooper."

ANTHONY QUINN

He once dated a mother and daughter simultaneously. And he became a father at the age of 78…

JOHN BARRYMORE

Liked brothels so much that, he even rented one for a month when he was in Calcutta, familiarizing himself with all thirty-nine positions of the *Kama Sutra* at the insistence of his obliging hostesses.

LONG DAY'S JOURNEY INTO NIGHT
15 films that run and run

1900, 1977 (311 minutes)
Cleopatra, 1963 (251 minutes)
Napoleon, 1927 (235 minutes)
Gone with the Wind, 1939 (233 minutes)
Once Upon a Time in America, 1984 (227 minutes)
Heaven's Gate, 1980 (220 minutes)
Exodus, 1960 (213 minutes)
Ben Hur, 1959 (211 minutes)

Nixon, 1995 (191 minutes)
JFK, 1991 (189 minutes)
Gandhi, 1982 (187 minutes)
The Longest Day, 1962 (183 minutes)
The Deer Hunter, 1978 (183 minutes)
Tess, 1980 (180 minutes)
Around the World in Eighty Days, 1956 (180 minutes)

M

FACE/OFF
10 makeup challenges

FRANCESCA ANNIS in *Krull* (1982)
Eleven layers of latex compound were used on her face to
transform her into a 100-year-old woman. It took eight
and a half hours' work per day and prevented her from eating.

JOHN HURT in *The Elephant Man* (1980)
A seven-hour ordeal that was so exhausting that it was only
undertaken every second day.

BORIS KARLOFF in *The Bride of Frankenstein* (1935)
Seven hours of grueling work every day.

CHARLES LAUGHTON in *The Hunchback of Notre Dame* (1939)
Four and a half hours per day.

ROD STEIGER in *The Illustrated Man* (1969)
It took the makeup department thirty-four hours to tattoo his
whole body.

DUSTIN HOFFMAN in *Little Big Man* (1970)
Hoffman suffered for five hours a day under a fourteen-piece
latex mask and some steaming-hot makeup lamps to undergo the
transition from a 33-year-old actor to a 121-year-old Indian.
"I defy anyone to put on that makeup and not feel old," he said
afterward.

EDDIE MURPHY in *The Nutty Professor* (1996)
Murphy sat in his chair for four hours daily while makeup artist

Rick Baker applied latex, wigs, and a bodysuit modeled from a 400-pound man to transform him into the entire Klump family of five, both male and female.

ROBERT DE NIRO in *Mary Shelley's Frankenstein* (1994)
Nine hours' work daily (but eventually reduced to six and a half), as De Niro had his face grotesquely transformed with latex and prosthetics.

JOHN MILLS in *Ryan's Daughter* (1969)
Mills had dental reconstruction, a false nose, twisted mouth, shaved eyebrows, and a revamped hairdo for the part that won him a Best Supporting Actor Oscar.

MARLON BRANDO in *The Godfather* (1972)
Slicked-back hair, shoe polish under the eyes, and generous cheekfuls of tissue paper were all Brando used for the famous screen test he did for Francis Ford Coppola to secure the part that resuscitated his career.

SLEEPING WITH THE ENEMY
20 stars on marriage and divorce

"A man can have two, maybe three love affairs while he's married. After that you're cheating." (Yves Montand)

"Marriage is very difficult. Very few of us are fortunate enough to marry multimillionaire girls with thirty-nine-inch busts who have undergone frontal lobotomies." (Tony Curtis)

"Marriage requires a special talent, like acting. And monogamy requires genius." (Warren Beatty)

"Marriage is the best magician there is. In front of your eyes it can change a cute little dish into a boring dishwasher." (Ryan O'Neal)

"They say marriages are made in heaven. But so is thunder and lightning." (Clint Eastwood)

"Our marriage works because we both carry clubs of equal size." (Paul Newman)

"I was married by a judge. I should have asked for a jury." (Sylvester Stallone)

"I walked down the aisle as Conan the Barbarian and walked back up again as Arnold the Meek." (Arnold Schwarzenegger)

"In Hollywood, brides keep the bouquets and throw away the groom." (Groucho Marx)

"Dahling, this time I married a lawyer so he can handle the divorce." (Zsa Zsa Gabor)

"I was married once, in San Francisco. The great earthquake destroyed the marriage certificate—which proves that earthquakes aren't all bad." (W. C. Fields)

"Marriage is a great institution, but I'm not ready for an institution yet." (Mae West)

"I am a very committed wife. And I should be committed too—for being married so many times." (Elizabeth Taylor)

"I married a Kraut. Every night I get dressed up like Poland and he invades me." (Bette Midler)

"My mother gave me this advice: trust your husband; adore your husband…and get as much as you can in your own name." (Joan Rivers)

"My wife got the house, the car, the bank balance. And if I marry again and have children, she gets them too." (Woody Allen)

"You never realize how short a month is until after you pay alimony." (John Barrymore)

"If there's any realistic deterrent to marriage, it's the fact that you can't afford a divorce." (Jack Nicholson)

"The difference between divorce and legal separation is that a legal separation gives a husband time to hide his money." (Johnny Carson)

"Marriage is grand. Divorce is twenty grand." (Jay Leno)

JOBS FOR THE GIRLS
10 actresses who married directors

Brigitte Bardot (Roger Vadim)
Jamie Lee Curtis (Christopher Guest)
Isabella Rossellini (Martin Scorsese)
Anne Bancroft (Mel Brooks)
Nancy Allen (Brian De Palma)
Theresa Russell (Nicolas Roeg)
Rita Hayworth (Orson Welles)
Amy Irving (Steven Spielberg)
Julie Andrews (Blake Edwards)
Kate Winslet (Jim Threapleton)

BRIEF ENCOUNTERS
20 marriages that didn't last very long

Jean Arthur and Julian Ankar: 1 day
Rudolph Valentino and Jane Acker: 1 day
Dennis Hopper and Michelle Phillips: 8 days
Zsa Zsa Gabor and Felipe de Alba: 8 days
Patty Duke and Michael Tell: 13 days
Katharine Hepburn and Ludlow Ogden Smith: 3 weeks
Ernest Borgnine and Ethel Merman: 3 weeks
Gig Young and Kim Schmidt: 3 weeks
Gloria Swanson and Wallace Berry: 3 weeks
Debra Paget and Budd Boetticher: 22 days
Leif Erickson and Maggie Hayes: 1 month

Burt Lancaster and June Ernst: 1 month
Greer Garson and Edward Snelson: 5 weeks
Drew Barrymore and Jeremy Thomas: 6 weeks
Sammy Davis, Jr. and Loray White: 2 months
Carole Landis and Willis Hunt, Jr.: 2 months
James Caan and Sheila Ryan: 3 months
Richard Pryor and Flynn Belaise: 4 months
James Woods and Sarah Owen: 4 months
Ava Gardner and Artie Shaw: 7 months

THE MARRYING KIND
10 stars who got married repeatedly

JUDY GARLAND
Married five times in all. When she invited her daughter, Liza
Minnelli, to her fifth wedding, Minnelli replied, "I can't make it,
Mama, but I promise I'll come to your next one."

BRIGITTE BARDOT
Was married five times before she realized she preferred dogs.
"Men took their pleasure," she said, "and ran."

ZSA ZSA GABOR
Had nine husbands in all, causing Milton Berle to quip, "Every
woman in Beverly Hills is wondering what to get her husband
for Christmas. Zsa Zsa Gabor is wondering what husband to get
for Christmas."

LANA TURNER
Said her ambition in life was to have one husband and seven
children, but it worked out the other way around!

ELIZABETH TAYLOR

Married eight times. "Always the bride," as one wag put it, "never the bridesmaid."

JOHNNY CARSON

Married four times, with many fireworks. "You know why divorces cost so much?" he asks rhetorically, "because they're worth it!"

STAN LAUREL

Married eight times, but there were only four different women involved, as he married two of them three times each. His Russian bride Llemara claims he brought one of his ex'es on their honeymoon—and that he tried to dig her grave on another occasion.

AVA GARDNER

Married Artie Shaw, Mickey Rooney, and Frank Sinatra, but all three marriages hit the rocks. Not surprising, perhaps, when we consider her husbands had nineteen wives between them: Shaw with seven, Rooney with eight, and Sinatra with four.

BETTE DAVIS

Married four times. She said of her fourth husband Gary Merrill, "Gary was a macho man, but none of my husbands was ever man enough to become Mr. Bette Davis."

JANE WYMAN

Was married five times in all, including once to a future president (Ronald Reagan). "I recommend marriage highly," she said once, "to everyone but me."

MY FAVORITE WIFE
10 pairs who married each other twice

George C. Scott and Colleen Dewhurst
George Peppard and Elizabeth Ashley
Carroll O'Connor and Nancy Fields
Don Johnson and Melanie Griffith
Jane Wyman and Freddie Karger
David and Gail Carradine
Richard Burton and Elizabeth Taylor
Milton Berle and Joyce Mathews
Lucille Ball and Desi Arnaz
Robert Wagner and Natalie Wood

ADDICTED TO LOVE
10 male stars who married more than three times

Richard Pryor: 7
Claude Rains: 7
Louis Armstrong: 6
Johnny Weissmuller: 6
Rex Harrison: 6

Clark Gable: 5
Richard Burton: 5
Tony Curtis: 5
Milton Berle: 4
Charlie Chaplin: 4

WEDDING BELLES
10 female stars with equally high marriage tallies

Lana Turner: 7

Barbara Hutton: 7

Jennifer O'Neill: 7

Martha Raye: 6

Hedy Lamarr: 6

Gloria Swanson: 6

Rita Hayworth: 5

Ginger Rogers: 5

Joan Collins: 4

Doris Day: 4

DIRTY ROTTEN SCOUNDRELS
10 marriages rocked by adultery

DENNIS HOPPER

The ink was hardly dry on the license when his marriage to Michelle Phillips went bust. She went off with Leonard Cohen instead and called Hopper a week later to ask him if he had ever thought of suicide. He got the message that their relationship was in trouble at this point.

BRUCE WILLIS

Demi Moore filed for divorce in 1997 after allegedly finding Bruce in bed with one of their friends. They had been married for ten years.

DOLLY PARTON

Her marriage to Carl Dean has wobbled on amid tales of mutual philandering.

WHITNEY HOUSTON

Has tended to shut her eyes to husband Bobby Brown's extra-marital dalliances.

SEAN CONNERY
His wife Micheline has stood by him for twenty-three years in the face of nonstop rumors about his love trysts.

GARY COOPER
Had affairs with the Magnificent Seven—Anita Ekberg, Grace Kelly, Ingrid Bergman, Clara Bow, Marlene Dietrich, Carole Lombard, and Tallulah Bankhead—but still wouldn't leave his wife. In fact, Rocky had such tolerance of his philandering ways that she often let him stay at a separate hotel from hers when they were on vacation together.

RICHARD BURTON
Used to book double hotel rooms for himself and Elizabeth Taylor when they were married, because their shouting matches were so loud they didn't want to annoy people who might be occupying the neighboring rooms.

MICHAEL DOUGLAS
Checked himself into rehab in 1992 to battle sex addiction after his wife Diandra caught him in bed with one of her best friends. (They were divorced in 1995 after eighteen years of marriage.)

KEVIN COSTNER
Divorced from his wife of sixteen years, Cindy, after she got wind of his dalliance with a Hawaiian hula dancer (among others). Cost: $40 million.

PAMELA ANDERSON
Filed for divorce from Tommy Lee in 1997 amid tales of his spousal abuse. She even removed tattoos of his name from various parts of her person. Bizarrely, they're now back together. But for how long?

TWO-OSCAR FAMILY

5 married couples who were both Academy Award-nominated

Laurence Olivier and Vivien Leigh
Kenneth Branagh and Emma Thompson
Richard Burton and Elizabeth Taylor
Tom Cruise and Nicole Kidman
Paul Newman and Joanne Woodward

(Only Tom Cruise failed to win.)

KEEP IT IN THE FAMILY

5 married couples nominated for Oscars in the same year

Alfred Lunt and Lynne Fontaine in 1931, both for *The Guardsman*.

Frank Sinatra and Ava Gardner in 1953, for *From Here to Eternity* and *Mogambo*.

Charles Laughton and Elsa Lanchester in 1957, both for *Witness for the Prosecution*.

Rex Harrison and Rachel Roberts in 1963 for *Cleopatra* and *This Sporting Life*.

Richard Burton and Elizabeth Taylor in 1966, both for *Who's Afraid of Virginia Woolf?*

(The four lucky winners were Lunt, Fontaine, Sinatra and Taylor.)

ATTACK OF THE 50-FOOT WOMEN
10 actresses on men

"The only time a woman really succeeds in changing a man is when he's a baby." (Natalie Wood)

"Macho doesn't prove mucho." (Zsa Zsa Gabor)

"The reason the all-American boy prefers beauty to brains is because the all-American boy can see better than he can think." (Farrah Fawcett-Majors)

"It is possible that blondes also prefer gentlemen." (Mamie Van Doren)

"Men are those creatures with two legs and eight hands." (Jayne Mansfield)

"There aren't any hard women—just soft men." (Raquel Welch)

"All men are alike. If you ask any American man, 'How are you?' he'll answer, 'Fine,' even if his mother just had a heart attack." (Joan Hackett)

"The more I see of men, the more I like dogs." (Brigitte Bardot)

"Most men are one hell of an outlay with a very small return." (Glenda Jackson)

"A woman isn't complete without a man. But where do you find a real man these days?" (Lauren Bacall)

DOGS OF WAR
10 military heroes

AUDIE MURPHY
The most-decorated soldier in American history, he professed to have killed over 200 Germans in World War II.

JAMES STEWART
Retired from the U.S. Air Force in 1968 after serving twenty-seven years as brigadier general.

ERROL FLYNN
Claimed to have fought alongside Fidel Castro in Cuba in 1959 …but was also accused of being a Nazi spy.

GENE AUTRY
Fought as a cargo pilot during World War II.

AL JOLSON
Purportedly the first American singer to entertain the troops in Korea, where he represented the UN.

GLENN FORD
Served in Vietnam, where he was shot down twice in a helicopter, and was also a captain in the U.S. Naval Reserves.

ERNEST BORGNINE
Worked in the U.S. Navy for ten years before becoming an actor.

KRIS KRISTOFFERSON
A former helicopter pilot in the army before he turned to music and acting.

CLIFF ROBERTSON
A former merchant marine, his ship was bombed in the Pacific shortly after the invasion of Pearl Harbor, an incident uncannily similar to the sinking of PT 109 some years later when Robertson immortalized it, playing John F. Kennedy in the movie of that name.

CLARK GABLE
Received a medal for a series of bombing missions he took part in during the World War II.

YOU DON'T SAY
5 famous misquotations

Humphrey Bogart never said, "Play it again, Sam" in *Casablanca* (1942). What he actually said was, "Play it, Sam. If she can take it, I can."

Neither did James Cagney ever say, "You dirty rat"—well not like that anyway. He said, "You dirty double-crossing rat," in *Blonde Crazy* (1931) and "You dirty yellow-bellied rat," in *Taxi* (1932).

Mae West eventually said, "Come up and see me sometime," but her first utterance of the line in *She Done Him Wrong* (1932) was "Come up sometime and see me."

Neither did Charles Boyer ever say "Come wiz me to ze Casbah" in *Algiers* (1938).

And nor did Greta Garbo say, "I want to be alone." The actual line was "I want to be left alone," in *Grand Hotel*, (1932).

AS GOOD AS IT GETS
the 10 biggest moneymaking films of all time

1. *Titanic* (1997) £1800 million
2. *Harry Potter and the Philosopher's Stone* (2001) £967 million
3. *Star Wars: The Phantom Menace* (1999) £923 million
4. *Jurassic Park* (1993) £881 million
5. *Lord of the Rings: Two Towers* (2002) £866 million
6. *Harry Potter and the Chamber of Secrets* (2002) £865 million
7. *Lord of the Rings: Fellowship of the Rings* (2001) £860 million
8. *Independence Day* (1996) £811 million
9. *Spider Man* (2002) £805 million
10. *Star Wars* (1977) £798 million

GIVE US THIS DAY OUR DAILY BREAD
10 more money facts

KIM BASINGER
Bought a town in Georgia for $20 million.

SHIRLEY TEMPLE
Was a millionairess before she was 10.

ALFRED HITCHCOCK
When he borrowed money, he insisted on returning it in coins.

W. C. FIELDS
Had hundreds of bank accounts throughout America and other parts of the world, which he opened under false names in order to hide his assets from the IRS. He was even known to get off trains which were making short stops at stations, to open accounts in new banks. He kept a special account in a German bank during World War II "in case that little bastard wins."

Star Wars: The Phantom Menace (1999)
George Lucas sold the merchandising rights alone for $100 million.

Star Trek (1980)
The closing credits cost more than the total combined cost of *Friday the 13th* and *Airplane*.

PETER FALK
Bought his trademark trench coat for $20 in 1967.

WARREN BEATTY
After Beatty discussed the egalitarian philosophy of John Reed with a group of extras during the filming of *Reds* (1981), they went on strike for higher wages!

JACK NICHOLSON
Cry Baby Killer (1958), his first film, was made on a budget of
$7,000 in ten days.

HOWARD HUGHES
Spent $12 million trying to buy up every copy of *The Conqueror*
(1953), which only cost $6 million to make.

MARILYN MONROE
10 cases for the prosecution

"A vacuum with nipples." (Otto Preminger)

"A woman who's unable to take refuge even in her own
insignificance." (Columbia Studios résumé)

"She's just an arrogant little tail-twitcher who's learned to throw
sex in your face." (Nunnally Johnson)

"She was good at playing abstract confusion in the same way
that a midget is good at being short." (Clive James)

"Wave a script in front of her and she comes down with a cold."
(Darryl F. Zanuck)

"There's a broad with a big future behind her." (Constance Bennett)

"She moves her upper lip around like a snake." (Howard Hughes)

"Directing her was like directing Lassie: it took fourteen takes to
get the bark right." (Billy Wilder)

"I said to her on the the set once, 'Why can't you get here on time, for fuck's sake?' And she replied, 'Oh! Do you have that word in England too?'" (Laurence Olivier)

"Working with Marilyn in *The Misfits* (1961) nearly gave me a heart attack. I have never been happier when a film ended." (Clark Gable)

10 CASES FOR THE DEFENSE

"She had the mysterious unfathomableness of a Garbo." Joshua Logan

"Anyone can remember lines, but it takes a real actress to come on the set not knowing her lines and give the performances she did." Billy Wilder

"Every time a director yelled 'Action' she'd break out in a sweat." Robert Mitchum

"She was like a ripe bowl of peaches." Anne Baxter

"A natural with no technique." George Axelrod

"She was the only gal who ever came close to me in the sex-appeal department. All the others had were big boobs." Mae West

"They treated her like a bubblehead, but she was very sharp." John Springer

"She was the most marvelous person I ever worked with."
Montgomery Clift

"She had a kind of fantastic beauty like Gloria Swanson, and she
radiated sex like Jean Harlow. She didn't need a soundtrack to
tell a story." Leon Shamroy

"You don't have to hold an inquest to find out who killed
Marilyn Monroe. Those bastards in the big executive chairs
killed her." Henry Hathaway

MONUMENTAL ROLES
5 famous monuments in movies

MOUNT RUSHMORE (*North by Northwest*, 1959)
Cary Grant and Eva Marie Saint hang onto it for grim death in
Hitchcock's classic.

THE EMPIRE STATE BUILDING (*King Kong*, 1933)
Provides the perfect roost on which to play with Fay Wray and
swat biplanes.

THE WHITE HOUSE (*Independence Day*, 1997)
Aliens make matchwood of the presidential home.

THE STATUE OF LIBERTY (*Planet of the Apes*, 1967)
Provides a startling finale, when Charlton Heston discovers the
ape planet is in fact his own.

BIG BEN (*The Thirty-Nine Steps*, 1978)
Robert Powell hangs from the clockface of Big Ben in an
attempt to make time stand still.

WHAT'S IN A NAME?
10 pieces of name trivia

ARNOLD SCHWARZENEGGER
The literal translation of his surname is "black plowshare."

TUESDAY WELD
She was actually born on a Friday.

SHIRLEY MACLAINE
Was named after Shirley Temple.

ROBIN WILLIAMS
Has two children called Zachary and Zelda.

GERARD DEPARDIEU
The literal translation of his surname is "Oh my God".

KYLIE MINOGUE
Her first name means "boomerang".

MICHAEL CAINE
Was called Old Snake Eyes in his youth because he never blinked.

SOPHIA LOREN
Was so thin as a child that she was nicknamed Toothpick.

JOAN CRAWFORD
Louis B. Mayer made her drop her real name, Lucille Le Sueur, because it sounded too much like "sewer." (He also thought Greta Garbo's last name sounded too much like "garbage" but this lady proved durable.)

WOODY ALLEN
Woody, who was born Allen Konigsberg, made his original Christian name into his film surname.

10 ACTORS WHO CHANGED THEIR NAMES

ROCK HUDSON
His real name was Roy Fitzgerald. Hudson came from the river and the rock from the Rock of Gibraltar. When Humphry Bogart met him he said acerbically, "You look very soft for a rock."

MICHAEL CAINE
Changed his name from Maurice Joseph Micklewhite to Michael Scott, and then to Michael Caine – after seeing a billboard advertising the film *The Caine Mutiny*. As he says "Michael Caine sounded a helluva lot better than Michael Mutiny."

RUDOLPH VALENTINO
His real name was (sharp intake of breath) Rodolpho Alphonzo Rafaelo Pierre Filibert Gugliemi di Valentina d'Antonguolla.

NICOLAS CAGE
His real name is Nicholas Coppola. He changed it to low-profile the connection with his uncle (Francis Ford Coppola) for fear of accusations of nepotism if and when he got ahead.

CHARLES BRONSON
Was born Charles Buchinski. Bronson came from the name of a street he was passing in his car one day when the lights went red.

RICHARD BURTON
His real name was Richard Jenkins.

TONY CURTIS
He was born Bernie Schwartz on New York's Lower East Side.

KIRK DOUGLAS
He was born Issur Danielovitch Demsky also in New York City.

STEWART GRANGER

His real name was James Stewart but Actor's Equity already had another James Stewart on their books so he had to change it.

MICHAEL KEATON

His real name was Michael Douglas. Guess why he changed it?

10 ACTRESSES WHO CHANGED THEIR NAMES

SIGOURNEY WEAVER

She was born Susan Weaver. She took the Sigourney from a character in *The Great Gatsby* because it was "long and curvy."

BETTE DAVIS

Her real first name was Ruth. The Bette came from Balzac's novel *Cousin Bette*.

DORIS DAY

This sounds a little more succinct than Doris von Kappelhoff, the name on her birth certificate. She chose it as a kind of thank you to a song that has been good to her: "Day After Day."

CAROLE LOMBARD

Born plain Jane Peters, she got Carole Lombard from the Carroll Lombardi pharmacy in New York.

BO DEREK

Her actual name is Cathleen Collins—not very exotic for a sex-kitten. Hence the metamorphosis.

MARILYN MONROE

She was born Norma Jean Mortenson. Monroe was her mother's maiden name.

DIANE KEATON
Her real name is Diane Hall, which is one reason why the movie
Annie Hall means so much to her.

JUDY GARLAND
Would she have become the most famous child star of her day if
she had stuck with her given name: Frances Gumm?

MADONNA
This is a shortened form of Madonna Louise Veronica Ciccone.

JENNIFER ANISTON
Born Jennifer Anistonopoulos, she clipped the end for under-
standable reasons.

15 STARS WHO USED THEIR MIDDLE NAME AS THEIR FIRST ONE

Edith (Norma) Shearer
Ernestine (Jane) Russell
John (Anthony) Quinn
Edward (Montgomery) Clift
Henry (Warren) Beatty
Charles (Robert) Redford
Robert (Oliver) Reed
Michael (Sylvester) Stallone
Dorothy (Faye) Dunaway
Maria (Debra) Winger
Walter (Stacy) Keach
Muriel (Teresa) Wright
George (Richard) Chamberlain
William (Brad) Pitt
William (Clark) Gable

10 STARS WHO CHANGED THEIR CHRISTIAN NAMES

Lana Turner (Julia)

Zsa Zsa Gabor (Sari)

Oliver Hardy (Norvell)

Bob Hope (Leslie)

Groucho Marx (Julius)

Kim Novak (Marilyn)

Van Heflin (Emmet Ryan)

Gary Cooper (Frank James)

Christopher Walken (Ronald)

Mickey Rourke (Philip)

10 STARS WHO USE THEIR MIDDLE NAME

Jamie Lee Curtis

Mary Louise Parker

Leslie Ann Warren

Jennifer Jason Leigh

Mary Ann Mobley

Mary Tyler Moore

Mary Beth Hurt

Harry Dean Stanton

Mary Kay Place

Tommy Lee Jones

35 OTHER NAME CHANGERS

Dean Martin (Dino Crocetti)

Cary Grant (Archibald Leech)

Kirk Douglas (Issur Danielovitch)

Edward G. Robinson (Emmanuel Goldberg)

Roy Rogers (Leonard Syle)

Julie Andrews (Julia Elizabeth Wells)

Lauren Bacall (Betty Joan Perske)

Susan Hayward (Edythe Marrener)

Rita Hayworth (Margarita Cansino)
Sophia Loren (Sofia Scicolone)
Demi Moore (Demi Guynes)
Angie Dickinson (Angeline Brown)
Susan Sarandon (Susan Tomaling)
Whoopi Goldberg (Caryn Johnson)
Cyd Charisse (Tula Elice Finklea)
Stan Laurel (Arthur Stanley Jefferson)
Cher (Cherilyn Sarkisian La Pierre)
Catherine Deneuve (Catherine Dorléac)
Peter Lorre (Lazlo Loewenstein)
Karl Malden (Malden Sekulovich)
Anouk Aimée (Françoise Sorya Dreyfus)
Goldie Hawn (Goldie Studlendgehawn)
Theresa Russell (Theresa Paup)
Winona Ryder (Winona Horowitz)
Tom Cruise (Thomas Cruise Mapother IV)
Ann Margret (Ann Margaret Olsson)
Elliott Gould (Elliott Goldstein)
Christian Slater (Christian Hawkins)
Emily Lloyd (Emily Lloyd-Pack)
Gene Wilder (Jerry Silberman)
Walter Matthau (Walter Matasschanskayasky)
Laurence Harvey (Laruska Mischa)
William Holden (William Beedle)
Nicolas Cage (Nicolas Kim Coppola)
Rudolph Valentino (Rodolfo Pietro Filiberto Raffaello Guglielmi di Valentina)

NEPOTISM

5 stars whose lovers or wives just "happened" to be in their movies

CHARLES BRONSON
Worked with Jill Ireland on:
The Valachi Papers (1972), *Chato's Land* (1972), *The Mechanic* (1972), *Breakheart Pass* (1976), *From Noon Till Three* (1976), *Love and Bullets* (1979), *Death Wish 2* (1982), *Assassination* (1986)

JOHN CASSAVETES
Worked with Gena Rowlands on:
A Child is Waiting (1963), *Faces* (1968), *Minnie and Moskovitz* (1971), *A Woman Under the Influence* (1974), *Two Minute Warning* (1976), *Opening Night* (1977), *Gloria* (1980), *Love Streams* (1984)

CLINT EASTWOOD
Worked with Sondra Locke on:
The Outlaw Josey Wales (1976), *The Gauntlet* (1977), *Every Which Way But Loose* (1978), *Bronco Billy* (1980), *Every Which Way You Can* (1980), *Sudden Impact* (1983)

WOODY ALLEN
Worked with Mia Farrow on:
A Midsummer Night's Sex Comedy (1982), *Zelig* (1983), *Broadway Danny Rose* (1984), *The Purple Rose of Cairo* (1985), *Hannah and Her Sisters* (1985), *Radio Days* (1987), *September* (1987), *Crimes and Misdemeanors* (1990), *Shadows and Fog* (1991), *Husbands and Wives* (1992).

BLAKE EDWARDS
Worked with Julie Andrews on:
Darling Lili (1970), *The Tamarind Seed* (1974), *10* (1979), *S.O.B.* (1981), *Victor/Victoria* (1982), *The Man Who Loved Women* (1983), *That's Life* (1986)

WRITTEN ON THE WIND
10 stars who've written novels

Whoopi Goldberg (*Alice*)
Julie Andrews (*The Last of the Really Great Whangdoodles*)
Tony Curtis (*Kid Andrew Cody and Julie Sparrow*)
Joan Collins (*Prime Time*)
Robert Shaw (*The Sun Doctor*)
David Niven (*Once Over Lightly*)
Dirk Bogarde (*West of Sunset*)
Simon Signoret (*Adieu Volidia*)
Mae West (*The Constant Sinner*)
Jean Harlow (*Today is Tonight*)

5 DIRECTORS WHO'VE WRITTEN NOVELS

Orson Welles (*Mr. Arkadin*)
John Sayles (*Union Dues*)
Jean Cocteau (*Les Enfants Terribles*)
Gus Van Sant (*Pink*)
Pier Paolo Pasolini (*A Violent Life*)

GRIN AND BARE IT
10 star nudity quotes

"Nobody gives a monkey's uncle about nudity today be it a male or female, unless you've got three tits." David Hemmings

"I've got nothing against it…We're born this way." Ursula Andress

"Nudity in the flesh doesn't bother me, but having my mind uncovered scares the hell out of me." Margot Kidder

"My breasts aren't actresses." Liv Ullmann

"I'm not a tiny woman. When Sophia Loren is naked, there is a lot of nakedness." Sophia Loren

"I think nudity is disgusting. But if I were 22, with a great body, it would be artistic, tasteful, patriotic, and a progressively religious experience." Shelley Winters

"A woman's ass is for her husband, not theatregoers."
Louis B. Mayer

"I'm never naked in front of a lens. I can't be mixed up with those little whores that undress at any moment. My father and mother would only allow me to see the films of Shirley Temple when I was young." Gina Lollobrigida

"It's traditional when you run out of creative juices to go to the old dropping-the-pants routine." June Havoc

"When I'm cleaning the house I wear an apron, but nothing else. It makes my activities more interesting for my husband." Nina Foch

BOTTOMS UP
10 nude male fannies on display

Mel Gibson, *Lethal Weapon* (1987)
Kevin Costner, *Dances with Wolves* (1990)
Richard Gere, *American Gigolo* (1979)
Matt Dillon, *A Kiss Before Dying* (1991)
Michael Douglas, *Fatal Attraction* (1987)
Arnold Schwarzenegger, *Total Recall* (1990)
Dennis Quaid, *The Big Easy* (1987)
Mickey Rourke, *Angel Heart* (1987)
Oliver Reed, *Women in Love* (1969)
Jack Nicholson, *Something's Got to Give* (2004)

THE WAY THEY WERE

30 former occupations of actors

JACK LEMMON
Beer-hall pianist

CHARLTON HESTON
Nude model for an Art Student League in New York, at a rate of
$1.25 an hour

DAVID LYNCH
Garbage collector, animal dissector, and deliverer of the *Wall
Street Journal*

ROBERT MITCHUM
Circus horseback rider, heavyweight boxer, and a spy behind the
German lines during World War II

ANTHONY QUINN
Shoeshiner in front of a church

GABRIEL BYRNE
Spent four years studying to be a priest, becoming addicted to
drinking altar wine and eating congealed grease in the process.

PAUL NEWMAN
Picked up golf balls and cleaned them for reuse

ROBERT REDFORD
Parisian sidewalk artist

ERROL FLYNN
Was once a slave trader in New Guinea, where he rounded up
natives to be sold into bondage as plantation workers. He also
worked on a sheep farm in Queensland, castrating lambs by
biting off their testicles.

JACK NICHOLSON
Sorted out fan mail for Tom and Jerry

ALAN ALDA
Clown, taxicab driver, doorman

BEN KINGSLEY
Penicillin tester

STAN LAUREL
Charlie Chaplin's understudy

BURT LANCASTER
Acrobat, lingerie salesman

SYLVESTER STALLONE
Trainee beautician

WARREN BEATTY
Rat-catcher

MICHAEL CAINE
Meat porter

ELVIS PRESLEY
Truck driver, movie theater usher

ALEC GUINNESS
Advertising copywriter

ALAN LADD
Hot-dog-stand proprietor

SEAN CONNERY
French polisher for coffin maker

CARY GRANT
Sandwich man on stilts

BURT REYNOLDS
Ballroom bouncer

ROGER MOORE
Model for knitting patterns

LEE MARVIN
Septic tank cleaner

GABRIEL BYRNE
Plumber's assistant

ROCK HUDSON
Vacuum cleaner salesman

RONALD REAGAN
Lifeguard

RAYMOND BURR
Shepherd

WALTER MATTHAU
Filing clerk

15 FORMER OCCUPATIONS OF ACTRESSES

MARILYN MONROE
Stripper, aircraft factory worker

RAQUEL WELCH
Secretary to a bishop

DOROTHY LAMOUR
Door-to-door radio saleswoman

BARBARA STANWYCK
Package wrapper

AUDREY HEPBURN
Dental assistant

GOLDIE HAWN
Go-go dancer

LANA TURNER
Usherette

LAUREN BACALL
Lingerie shop assistant

JAYNE MANSFIELD
Saucepan saleswoman

BARBRA STREISAND
Switchboard operator

ROSEANNE
Chef

GLENDA JACKSON
Shop assistant in a pharmacy

GRETA GARBO
Soap latherer in a barbershop

JANE RUSSELL
Chiropodist's assistant

GRACE KELLY
Model for insecticide

SUNSET BOULEVARD
15 stars' post-movie occupations

MYRNA LOY
Took up a post with the UN.

GINA LOLLOBRIGIDA
Became an unlikely journalist, at one time even getting to interview Fidel Castro.

MAUREEN O'HARA
Vice-president of an airline company

CARY GRANT
Executive in a cosmetics firm

JANICE RULE
Entered psychoanalysis—as doctor rather than patient. (But most of her clients came from the acting profession, not surprisingly.)

RICHARD TODD
Dairy farmer

AUDREY HEPBURN
Goodwill Ambassador for UNICEF

JANE WYMAN
Painter

JANE RUSSELL
Founded an agency for American couples wishing to adopt foreign children.

DOLORES HART
The former costar of Elvis Presley became a nun.

VERONICA LAKE
Ended her life as a barmaid in a New York hotel.

BUSTER CRABBE
Stockbroker

JAMES FOX
Evangelist

RODDY MCDOWALL
Photographer

RICHARD BEYMER
Taught transcendental meditation in L.A.

LIGHTS, CAMERA, ACTION!
10 memorable opening lines of movies

"Most of what follows is true."
Butch Cassidy and the Sundance Kid, 1969

"And so they lived happily ever after. Or did they?"
The Palm Beach Story, 1942

"For those who believe in God, no explanation is necessary.
For those who do not, no explanation is possible."
The Song of Bernadette, 1943

"This picture is dedicated to all the beautiful women in the
world who have shot their husbands full of holes." *Roxie Hart*,
1942

"Hey, boy, what you doin' with my momma's car?"
Bonnie and Clyde, 1967

"What can you say about a 25-year-old girl that died?"
Love Story, 1970

"On November 1, 1959, the population of New York City was
8,042,783." *The Apartment*, 1960

"Last night I dreamed I went to Manderley again." *Rebecca*,
1940

"Yes, this is Sunset Boulevard, Los Angeles, California."
Sunset Boulevard, 1950

"I believe in America." *The Godfather*, 1972

UNCLE OSCAR
5 Oscar facts

1. It's 13½ inches high.
2. It's cast in solid Britannia metal electroplated with 28 karat gold.
3. It weighs 8½ pounds.
4. It's worth approximately $400. But if you want to sell it, you first have to offer it back to the Academy of Motion Picture Arts and Sciences.
5. The name Oscar itself was conceived by director Margaret Herrick, who observed that the little statues reminded her of her uncle Oscar.

SWEEPING THE BOARDS
10 films that have won eight or more Oscars

Ben Hur (11), 1959
Titanic (11), 1998
West Side Story (10), 1961
Gigi (9), 1958
The Last Emperor (9), 1987
The English Patient (9), 1996
Gone with the Wind (8), 1939
From Here To Eternity (8), 1953
On the Waterfront (8), 1954
My Fair Lady (8), 1964

DOUBLE WHAMMY
5 actors who've won two Oscars

MARLON BRANDO*
On the Waterfront (1954), *The Godfather* (1972)

TOM HANKS
Philadelphia (1993), *Forrest Gump* (1994)

DUSTIN HOFFMAN
Kramer vs. Kramer (1979), *Rain Man* (1988)

GARY COOPER
Sergeant York (1941), *High Noon* (1952)

FREDERIC MARCH
Dr. Jekyll and Mr. Hyde (1932), *The Best Years of Our Lives* (1946)

(*Brando, of course, refused his second Oscar because of his objections to Hollywood's depiction of Native Americans.)

THIRD TIME LUCKY
5 actors nominated for Oscars in three successive years

SPENCER TRACY (1936–8)
San Francisco, Captains Courageous, Boystown

GARY COOPER (1941–3)
Sergeant York, The Pride of the Yankees, For Whom the Bell Tolls

GREGORY PECK (1945–7)
Keys of the Kingdom, The Yearling, Gentleman's Agreement

RICHARD BURTON (1964–6)
Becket, The Spy Who Came in from the Cold, Who's Afraid of Virginia Woolf?

JACK NICHOLSON (1973–5)
The Last Detail, Chinatown, One Flew over the Cuckoo's Nest

(Tracy won for *Captains Courageous* and *Boystown*; Cooper, for *Sergeant York;* and Nicholson, for *One Flew over the Cuckoo's Nest.*)

LADIES CHOICE
5 actresses nominated in successive years

INGRID BERGMAN (1943–5)
For Whom the Bell Tolls, Gaslight, The Bells of St. Mary's

DEBORAH KERR (1956–8)
The King and I, Heaven Knows Mr. Allison, Separate Tables

JANE FONDA (1977–9)
Julia, Coming Home, The China Syndrome

MERYL STREEP (1981–3)
The French Lieutenant's Woman, Sophie's Choice, Silkwood

GLENN CLOSE (1987–8)
Fatal Attraction, Dangerous Liaisons

(Bergman won for *Gaslight*; Fonda, for *Coming Home;* and Streep, for *Sophie's Choice.*)

UNDERSTUDY ACHIEVERS
10 Oscars won by second-choice leads

Greer Garson in *Mrs. Miniver* (1942). Norma Shearer refused the role because she that felt she was too old.

Grace Kelly in *The Country Girl* (1954) after Greta Garbo said no.

Jodie Foster in *Silence of the Lambs* (1991), a role that Michelle Pfeiffer snubbed.

Lee Marvin in *Cat Ballou* (1965), after Kirk Douglas refused to take it on.

Joanne Woodward in *The Three Faces of Eve* (1957) after Eva Marie Saint refused the part.

Charlton Heston in *Ben Hur* (1959). The most famous role of his career, but Burt Lancaster had first bite of the cherry.

Donna Reed in *From Here to Eternity* (1953), replaced first-choice Julie Harris.

Louise Fletcher in *One Flew over the Cuckoo's Nest* (1975), only secured the role after actresses like Angela Lansbury, Coleen Dewhurst, Anne Bancroft and Geraldine Page cried off.

Gary Cooper in *High Noon* (1952), after Gregory Peck refused the part.

Peter Finch in *Network* (1976). He won a posthumous Oscar after Henry Fonda took a rain check on the role of the loopy broadcaster.

HERE'S TO THE LOSERS

10 great actors who never won Oscars

Peter O'Toole
Kirk Douglas
Robert Mitchum
Orson Welles
Montgomery Clift

Steve McQueen
Peter Sellers
W. C. Fields
Charlie Chaplin
Richard Burton

10 GREAT ACTRESSES WHO NEVER WON OSCARS

Greta Garbo
Barbara Stanwyck
Marlene Dietrich
Jean Harlow
Marilyn Monroe

Judy Garland
Natalie Wood
Rita Hayworth
Gloria Swanson
Lana Turner

10 NON-OSCAR WINNERS WITH THE MOST NOMINATIONS

Richard Burton (7)
Peter O'Toole (7)
Deborah Kerr (6)
Thelma Ritter (6)
Arthur Kennedy (5)

Glenn Close (5)
Alfred Hitchcock (5)
Mickey Rooney (4)
Albert Finney (4)
Marsha Mason (4)

HIS AND HERS
5 films which won best actor and actress Oscars

It Happened One Night (1934)
Clark Gable and Claudette Colbert

One Flew over the Cuckoo's Nest (1975)
Jack Nicholson and Louise Fletcher

On Golden Pond (1981)
Katharine Hepburn and Henry Fonda

Silence of the Lambs (1991)
Anthony Hopkins and Jodie Foster

As Good as It Gets (1998)
Jack Nicholson and Helen Hunt

PHENOMINATIONS
10 films with the highest Oscar nomination tally (number actually won in brackets)

All About Eve: 14 (6)
Titanic: 14 (11)
Lord of the Rings 13 (13)
Gone with the Wind: 13 (8)
From Here to Eternity: 13 (8)
Forrest Gump: 13 (6)
Mary Poppins: 13 (5)
Who's Afraid of Virginia Woolf?: 13 (5)
Dances with Wolves: 12 (7)
Mrs. Miniver: 12 (6)

(If you're feeling sorry for *Johnny Belinda,* spare a thought for the unluckiest two films in Oscars' history. 1977's *The Turning Point*, was nominated for eleven Oscars and won…none. *The Color Purple* suffered the same ignominy in 1985.)

HEAVEN CAN WAIT
10 very old Oscar winners

JESSICA TANDY
80 when she won for *Driving Miss Daisy* (1989)

GEORGE BURNS
80 when he won for *The Sunshine Boys* (1975)

MELVYN DOUGLAS
79 when he won for *Being There* (1979)

JOHN GIELGUD
77 when he won for *Arthur* (1981)

DON AMECHE
77 when he won for *Cocoon* (1985)

PEGGY ASHCROFT
77 when she won for *A Passage to India* (1984)

HENRY FONDA
76 when he won for *On Golden Pond* (1981)

KATHARINE HEPBURN
74 when she won for *On Golden Pond* (1981)

EDMUND GWENN
72 when he won for *Miracle on 34th Street* (1947)

RUTH GORDON
72 when she won for *Rosemary's Baby* (1968)

CRADLE SNATCHERS
10 very young Oscar winners

SHIRLEY TEMPLE
Only 6 when she received a Special Oscar for Outstanding
Contribution to Movies in 1934.

MARGARET O'BRIEN
Received a special award for *Meet Me in St. Louis* (1944), aged 8.

VINCENT WINTER
Received a special award for *The Little Kidnappers* (1954), aged 6.

IVAN JANDL
Received a special award for *The Search* (1948), aged 9.

JON WHITLEY
Received a special award for *The Little Kidnappers* (1954),
aged 10.

TATUM O'NEAL
Won Best Supporting Actress for *Paper Moon* (1973), aged 10.

ANNA PAQUIN
Won Best Supporting Actress for *The Piano* (1993), aged 11.

CLAUDE JARMAN JR
Received a special award for *The Yearling* (1946), aged 12.

BOBBY DRISCOLL
Received a special award for *The Window* (1949), aged 12.

HAYLEY MILLS
Received a special award for *Pollyanna* (1960), aged 13.

MONKEY SEE, MONKEY DO
5 Oscar winners who are the children of stars

Anjelica Huston
Jane Fonda
Liza Minnelli
Michael Douglas
Tatum O'Neal

OSCAR WILD...
10 pieces of assorted Oscar trivia

After John Wayne won an Oscar for playing Rooster Cogburn in *True Grit* (1969), he commented, "If I knew it was that easy to win, I would've put on an eye patch thirty-five years ago."

Even though Hattie McDaniel won the Best Supporting Actress award for *Gone with the Wind* (1939), she was prohibited from attending the world première of the film, which was held in the racially segregated city of Atlanta.

Woody Allen refused to attend the Oscar ceremonies on the night he won a statuette for *Annie Hall* (1977): he was too busy playing the clarinet in a New York jazz bar on the night in question.

"All an award usually means," says Bob Hoskins, "is that you don't work for eighteen months because nobody thinks they can afford you."

When Frank Sinatra won the Oscar for *From Here to Eternity* (1953), he went for a walk with his new friend...and a policeman accused him of stealing it.

James Dean was the only actor to have been nominated for two posthumous Oscars—for *East of Eden* and *Giant* (1955 and 1956).

After a streaker interrupted the 1974 ceremonies, David Niven quipped, "Just think: the only laugh that man will probably ever get is for showing his shortcomings." The same man was subsequently murdered in a sex shop he owned in San Francisco.

Diane Ladd and her real-life daughter Laura Dern were both nominated for Oscars for the same film (*Rambling Rose*, 1991).

Three generations of the Huston family have won Oscars: Walter and John for *The Treasure of the Sierra Madre* (1948, acting and directing honors) and Anjelica for *Prizzi's Honor* (1985).

Elia Kazan's films have received a whopping total of sixty Oscar nominations in all.

OUTLAWED
5 things banned on screen by the Hays Code

1. Excessive or lustful kissing (anything over three seconds)
2. Mention of sexual hygiene or venereal diseases
3. Miscegenation—sex relationships between whites and blacks
4. The inside thigh of a female between the garter and panties
5. If two people appeared in bed together, one of them had to have a foot on the floor

P

BRINGING UP BABY
10 stars who had parenting problems

GREGORY PECK

His eldest son Jonathan looked a lot like him, but couldn't reach the same degree of success in life. He shot himself to death in 1975 after a lifetime of depression and ill health. Peck never forgave himself for not being there to see him through his crisis.

JOAN CRAWFORD

Terrorized her children by beating them with coat hangers among other things, as well as locking them in the linen closet with the lights out for minor misdemeanors. Christina wrote a book about it all called *Mommie Dearest* which was subsequently filmed with Faye Dunaway as the demented diva.

HENRY FONDA

Had a long-lasting war of attrition with Jane before they publicly kissed and made up on the set of *On Golden Pond* (1981).

MARLON BRANDO

His son Christian killed the fiancé of his daughter Cheyenne, who subsequently committed suicide.

MARTIN SHEEN

Used tough love to get Charlie off his drug habit. Charlie now tells us that his dad saved his life.

TONY CURTIS

Was too messed up with cocaine and bad movie parts to be a proper dad to Jamie Lee when it counted. "I got to know him through doing drugs with him," she tells us now.

VIC MORROW

Disliked his daughter Jennifer Jason Leigh so much that in his will—he was decapitated on the set of *Twilight Zone: The Movie* (1983)—he only left her $78.18. Meanwhile, $600,000, went to her sister Carrie Ann.

PAUL NEWMAN

Could never get close enough to his son Scott—who eventually committed suicide—to tell him that movie success wasn't what it was all about.

DEBBIE REYNOLDS

Nearly lost Carrie Fisher to drugs before she fought her way back from the brink.

KIRK DOUGLAS

"I would have been much nicer to him when he was a kid," Kirk said of Michael, "if I knew how successful he was going to become!"

THE PARENT TRAP
10 sets of parents and children in real (and reel) life

RYAN O'NEAL

Played the father of his daughter Tatum in *Paper Moon* (1973).

DEMI MOORE

The mother of her daughter Rumer in *Striptease* (1996).

DIANE CILENTO

The mother of her son Jason Connery (by Sean) in *The Boy Who Had Everything* (1984).

MICHAEL REDGRAVE
Father of Vanessa in *Behind the Mask* (1958).

HENRY FONDA
Father of Jane in his swansong role in *On Golden Pond* (1981).

ALAN LADD
Father of his son David in *The Proud Rebel* (1958).

CHARLTON HESTON
Father of his son Fraser in *The Ten Commandments* (1956).

MAUREEN O'SULLIVAN
Mother of her daughter Mia Farrow in Woody Allen's *Hannah and Her Sisters* (1986).

LAURA DERN
Daughter of her mother Diane Ladd, in *Wild at Heart* (1990).

OMAR SHARIF
Father of his real-life son Tarek in *Dr. Zhivago* (1965).

DOUBLE TROUBLE
15 stars who played two parts in films

Brad Pitt (*Meet Joe Black*, 1998)
Hayley Mills (*The Parent Trap*, 1961)
Dirk Bogarde (*Libel*, 1959)
Elvis Presley (*Kissin' Cousins*, 1964)
Sean Young (*A Kiss Before Dying*, 1991)
Mark Lester (*The Prince and the Pauper*, 1978)
Leonardo DiCaprio (*The Man in the Iron Mask*, 1998)
Jeremy Irons (*Dead Ringers*, 1988)
Jerry Lewis (*The Nutty Professor*, 1963)

Charlie Chaplin (*The Great Dictator*, 1940)
Lee Marvin (*Cat Ballou*, 1965)
Julie Christie (*Fahrenheit* 451, 1966)
Spencer Tracy (*Dr. Jekyll and Mr. Hyde*, 1941)
Meryl Streep (*The French Lieutenant's Woman*, 1981)
Olivia de Havilland (*The Dark Mirror*, 1946)

MULTIPLE PERSONALITY DISORDER
10 stars who played more than two parts in a film

Rolf Leslie, 27 parts (*Sixty Years a Queen*, 1913)
Lupino Lane, 24 parts (*Only Me*, 1929)
Joseph Henabery, 14 parts (*The Birth of a Nation*, 1915)
Robert Hirsch, 12 parts (*No Questions on Saturday*, 1964)
Michael Ripper, 9 parts (*What a Crazy World*, 1963)
Alec Guinness, 8 parts (*Kind Hearts and Coronets*, 1949)
Flavio Migliaccio, 8 parts (*Como Vai, Vai Bem*, 1969)
Rolv Wesenlund, 8 parts (*Norske Byggeklosser*, 1971)
Eddie Murphy, 5 parts (*The Nutty Professor*, 1963)
Peter Sellers, 3 parts (*Dr. Strangelove*, 1964)

SCREAM TOO
10 stars' phobias

GLENDA JACKSON
Suffers from claustrophobia.

JOAN COLLINS
Claims to be afraid of the dark.

MADONNA
Terrified of thunder.

HOWARD HUGHES
Had a pathological terror of any form of germs.

MARILYN MONROE
Suffered both from a fear of open spaces and also an apparently contradictory sensation that the world was closing in on her.

NATALIE WOOD
Had a lifelong fear of water, which was justified in the end: she drowned.

WHOOPI GOLDBERG
Hates flying so much, she says that she'd prefer to have her period.

MARLENE DIETRICH
Like Howard Hughes, she suffered from bacilophobia, the fear of germs.

KATHARINE HEPBURN
Had such a phobia about dirty hair that she used to go around movie sets sniffing people's heads.

JOAN CRAWFORD
Another clean freak. Was so obsessed with hygiene that she used to follow guests around her house wiping everything they touched—especially doorknobs.

NOBODY'S PERFECT
10 physical imperfections

REX HARRISON
Was blind in one eye.

MARLON BRANDO
Had his nose broken by Jack Palance in a boxing match, and never bothered to have it set, feeling he was "too beautiful" before.

HAROLD LLOYD
Lost the thumb and index finger of his right hand after a staged explosion went wrong on the set of one of his movies.

PETER FALK
Lost an eye at the age of 3 after an operation for a brain tumor.

RONALD REAGAN
Has suffered from partial deafness all his life since an actor fired a gun too close to him on a movie set at the beginning of his career.

HUMPHREY BOGART
His lip was scarred during the World War II when the troopship on which he was traveling was shelled by the Germans.

DUDLEY MOORE
Had a club foot.

CLINT EASTWOOD
Was once fired by Universal Studios because his Adam's apple stuck out too far.

MONTGOMERY CLIFT
Had a horrific car accident driving down a steep hill from Elizabeth Taylor's house, which disfigured his face on one side and altered his mind-set forever afterward.

MICHAEL J. FOX
Has Parkinson's Disease, but can see the funny side of it. As he says himself, "I can shake a Margharita in five seconds."

FROM CENTERFOLD TO CENTER STAGE

10 actresses who posed for Playboy

Marilyn Monroe

Margaux Hemingway

Joan Collins

Farrah Fawcett-Majors

Bo Derek

Catherine Deneuve

Sherilyn Fenn

Jayne Mansfield

Kim Basinger

Raquel Welch

ALL THE PRESIDENT'S MEN

5 politicians who appeared in movies

THEODORE ROOSEVELT
As himself in *Womanhood: The Glory of a Nation* (1917)

LEON TROTSKY
In *My Official Wife* (1914)

FIDEL CASTRO
As an extra in *Holiday in Mexico* (1946)

JOMO KENYATTA
Had a bit part in *Sanders of the River* (1935)

BENITO MUSSOLINI
As an extra in *The Eternal City* (1914)

THE CELLULOID JUKEBOX
15 stars who played pop stars in biopics

Dennis Quaid as Jerry Lee Lewis in *Great Balls of Fire* (1989)

Diana Ross as Billie Holiday in *Lady Sings the Blues* (1972)

Kurt Russell as Elvis Presley in *Elvis: The Movie* (1979)

Larry Parks as Al Jolson in *The Jolson Story* (1946)

Angela Bassett as Tina Turner in *What's Love Got to Do with It* (1993)

David Carradine as Woody Guthrie in *Bound for Glory* (1976)

Sissy Spacek as Loretta Lynn in *Coal Miner's Daughter* (1980)

Beverly D'Angelo as Patsy Cline in *Coal Miner's Daughter* (1980)

Forest Whitaker as Charlie Parker in *Bird* (1988)

Jessica Lange as Patsy Cline in *Sweet Dreams* (1985)

Gary Oldman as Sid Vicious in *Sid and Nancy* (1986)

Val Kilmer as Jim Morrison in *The Doors* (1991)

James Stewart as Glenn Miller in *The Glenn Miller Story* (1954)

Lou Diamond Phillips as Ritchie Valens in *La Bamba* (1987)

Ian Hart as John Lennon in *Backbeat* (1993)

JOHNNY GUITAR
10 pop stars in non-musical roles

JOHN LENNON
How I Won the War (1967)

ARLO GUTHRIE
Alice's Restaurant (1969)

MICK JAGGER
Performance (1970)

ART GARFUNKEL
Carnal Knowledge (1971)

BOB DYLAN
Pat Garrett and Billy the Kid (1973)

DIANA ROSS
Mahogany (1975)

DAVID BOWIE
The Man Who Fell to Earth (1976)

JANET JACKSON
Poetic Justice (1994)

STING
Brimstone and Treacle (1982)

LYLE LOVETT
The Player (1992)

FROM ONE STUDIO TO ANOTHER
10 pop stars who had simultaneous film careers

Elvis Presley	Cliff Richard
Frank Sinatra	Kris Kristofferson
Barbra Streisand	Madonna
Dean Martin	Doris Day
Liza Minnelli	Bing Crosby

HOLY CELLULOID, BATMAN
The Pope's 10 favorite films

Schindler's List (1993)
The harrowing multi-Oscar-winning drama

The Gospel According to St. Matthew (1964)
Unusual slant on the Bible, with Jesus portrayed as a rabid socialist

Life is Beautiful (1997)
A comic fable set in the Second World War

Modern Times (1936)
The last appearance of Charlie Chaplin as "the tramp"

Jesus of Nazareth (1977)
Franco Zeffirelli's sprawling six-hour epic

Ben Hur (1959)
Similar to a four-hour Sunday-school lesson

A Man for All Seasons (1966)
Endorsing the divine right of the Pope over and above his king

2001: A Space Odyssey (1968)
Stanley Kubrick's offbeat classic

8½ (1963)
Federico Fellini's autobiographical masterpiece

The Leopard (1963)
Luchino Visconti's personal meditation on the Sicilian aristocracy

THE NAKED TRUTH
5 stars who appeared in porn movies

SYLVESTER STALLONE
Made a movie called *Party at Kitty and Studs* (1970), getting paid $100 a day. When Stallone became famous, it was dusted off and shown at private parties for a $10,000 rental fee and renamed *The Italian Stallion*.

JOAN CRAWFORD
Made some sex movies back in the 1920s, most notably a silent one-reeler tantalizingly entitled *The Casting Couch*. It is alleged that after she became famous, MGM shelled out over half a million dollars in an attempt to buy up every surviving copy of the movie.

MALCOLM MCDOWELL
Caligula (1980), the $30-million epic bankrolled by Penthouse, has McDowell as the legendary emperor engaging in various forms of bestiality and incest as he writhes about the place in decidedly *fin-de-siècle* fashion with wife Helen Mirren et al. Gore Vidal worked on the script, but refused to allow his name to be used on the final credits.

KEVIN COSTNER
Appeared in a low-budget sexploitation flick called *Sizzle Beach* (1982).

MADONNA
When she was a struggling 19-year-old model, she appeared in *A Certain Sacrifice* (1978), which involves her in a rape scene in a coffee shop, an orgiastic dance session, and a ritual sacrifice.

COMING TO A THEATER NEAR YOU
30 great poster shoutlines

"Let's go to work." *Reservoir Dogs*, 1992

"Sex is power." *Disclosure*, 1994

"Four criminals. One line-up. No coincidence."
The Usual Suspects, 1995

"The next scream you hear may be your own."
Play Misty for Me, 1971

"You are cordially invited to George and Martha's for dinner."
Who's Afraid of Virginia Woolf? 1966

"She was the woman of Allen's dreams. She had large dark eyes, a beautiful smile…and a great pair of fins." *Splash*, 1984

"In space no one can hear you scream." *Alien*, 1979

"The hero is a berk." *Top Secret*, 1984

"Love means never having to say you're sorry." *Love Story*, 1970

"He's the last man on earth any woman needs…and every woman wants." *Breathless*, 1983

"Everything seemed so important then—even love!"
The Way We Were, 1973

"They came too late and stayed too long." *The Wild Bunch*, 1969

"Meet Benjamin. He's a little worried about his future."
The Graduate, 1967

"They're young, they're in love…and they kill people."
Bonnie and Clyde, 1967

"There are three sides to this love story."
Kramer vs. Kramer, 1979

"You don't assign him to cases—you just turn him loose!"
Dirty Harry, 1971

"Thou shalt not covet thy neighbor's wife."
Consenting Adults, 1992

"The coast is toast." *Volcano*, 1997

"The Greatest Motion Picture Ever Made."
Gone with the Wind, 1939

"In Vietnam the wind doesn't blow—it sucks."
Full Metal Jacket, 1987

"He's the kind of guy that every girl wants, but shouldn't marry!" *Cry-Baby*, 1990

"That Streetcar man has a new desire." *The Wild One*, 1954

"Don't give away the ending: it's the only one we have."
Psycho, 1960

"The dangerous age for women is from three to seventy."
Adam's Rib, 1949

"He treated her rough—and she loved it!" *Red Dust*, 1932

"Don't pronounce it—see it!" *Ninotchka*, 1939

"No one is as good as Bette when she's bad."
In This Our Life, 1942

"There never was a woman like Gilda." *Gilda*, 1946

"The story of a homosexual who married a nymphomaniac."
The Music Lovers, 1971

"The man with the barbed wire soul!" *Hud*, 1963

THE JOKER IS WILD
5 prank–players

ALFRED HITCHCOCK
Once bet a cameraman a large sum of money that he couldn't
spend the whole night alone in a dark studio. When the man took
him up on his offer, Hitchcock handcuffed him to a camera and
then gave him a large bottle of brandy to help pass the time.
What the cameraman didn't know was that Hitchcock had laced
it with laxatives, so it was quite a sight that greeted the rest of
the crew when they reported for work the next morning…

STAN LAUREL
At a dinner party with friends one evening, he pretended to
choke on a rabbit bone and vomit all over the room. He then
picked up what he had just thrown up and proceeded to re-eat it,
to the horror of his guests. He subsequently revealed a hot-water
bottle that he had hidden under his jacket, which was filled with
carrots and peas.

GRACE KELLY
Had a long-running practical joke going with Alec Guinness
whereby each would smuggle an Indian tomahawk into the
other's bed, no matter where they were. Part of the gag was that
neither would ever allude to the fact afterward.

MERVYN LEROY
The director of *Little Caesar* (1930) repeatedly nailed Edward G.
Robinson's cigars to wooden props during the making of the
movie, in order to watch Robinson's astounded reaction when he
went to light up.

RAOUL WALSH

On hearing of the death of John Barrymore, he bribed the funeral-parlor attendant, kidnapped the body, smuggled it into Errol Flynn's house, and sat it up in an armchair. When Flynn came home, drunk, he saw Barrymore sitting in his front room and let out a piercing scream.

R

REALITY BITES
fact versus fiction

CHRISTOPHER REEVE
Had already played a paraplegic on screen before the horrific
riding accident in 1994 that paralysed him for real.

DUSTIN HOFFMAN
During a break in filming *Tootsie* (1982), in which he played a
woman, he spent half an hour talking to fellow actor Jon Voight
without Voight realizing who he was.

ROBERT DE NIRO
Played a would-be assassin of a presidential candidate in *Taxi
Driver* (1976) opposite Jodie Foster. Foster's obsessive stalker
John Hinckley shot Ronald Reagan for real some years later, to
prove his love for her.

BOB HOSKINS
After playing Iago, he commented, "When you find you can play
a psychopath without too much effort, it's a bit worrying."

SHARON STONE
She said that the main problem about a screen image is that
eventually you start acting like it, and then you become it.

JOHN WAYNE
Was dying of cancer when he filmed *The Shootist* (1976),
featuring a character in the same situation.

CHARLIE CHAPLIN
He entered a Charlie Chaplin look-alike contest and came third.

MAGGIE SMITH
Won an Oscar for *California Suite* (1978), in which she played
an Oscar nominee.

R

WOODY ALLEN
Played a character who cheats on his wife with a much younger woman in *Crimes and Misdemeanors* (1989), just as Mia Farrow discovered that he was sleeping with Soon-Yi, the daughter she had adopted with her former husband André Previn.

JOHN TRAVOLTA
Plays a U.S. president who "invents" a war to distract attention from a sexual scandal in *Primary Colors* (1998). Not long after the movie was released, Bill Clinton was threatened with impeachment over an affair with Monica Lewinsky, and organized what many people believed to be unwarranted bomb strikes on Afghanistan and Sudan.

JOHN HUSTON
Says to Jack Nicholson in *Chinatown* (1974): "Are you sleeping with my daughter?" He means Faye Dunaway, his screen daughter, but at the time Nicholson was sleeping with Angelica, his real one.

AL CAPONE
Actually owned a copy of the Howard Hawks' version of *Scarface* (1932), which was loosely based on his own life. He threw a party for Hawks in Chicago immediately after the movie wrapped.

ROB LOWE
Immediately after making *Bad Influence* (1990), which centers on a character who finds himself in trouble after being video-taped in compromising sexual positions, Lowe landed in hot water after tapes of himself making love to underage girls in a hotel room surfaced and the mother of one of them sued.

GRACE KELLY
Her penultimate film role was as a princess in *The Swan* (1956). Shortly after making it, she became engaged to a prince in real life.

LEONARDO DICAPRIO

Two years after *Titanic* (1997), he was filming *The Beach* on
board a ship off the coast of Thailand when it sank and the cast
and crew had to head for the lifeboats.

RECORD-BREAKERS
20 movie records

The actor who credited himself with playing the most roles in a
career is Tom London. He appeared in more than 2,000 movies,
from his debut in *The Great Train Robbery* (1903) to his swansong in *The Lone Texan* (1959) fifty-six years later.

Indian comedienne Monomara worked on as many as thirty
movies at one time and made 1,000 in all. (The closest
Hollywood can come to that is John Wayne's 142.)

The actor with the longest movie career is the German performer
Curt Bois, who made his debut in 1908 at the age of 8 and
appeared finally in Wim Wenders' *Wings of Desire* (1988).
(America's Helen Hayes runs in at second with a seventy-eight-
year celluloid life span.)

The record for the most motion pictures made in any country in
one year goes to India, where a staggering 948 films were shot
in 1990.

The most costumes ever used in a film is 32,000 for *Quo Vadis*
(1951).

The most roles played by one actor in a film is twenty-seven. These were by Rolf Leslie in Will Barker's *Sixty Years a Queen* (1913), a biopic of Queen Victoria.

The most cameras ever used for a single scene was forty-eight, to film the sea battle in Fred Niblo's version of *Ben Hur* (1925).

The director with the longest Hollywood career is King Vidor, who started when he was 20 and was still roaring "Action" and "Cut" sixty-six years on.

A movie usher once boasted (confessed?) that he watched *Bedtime for Bonzo* (1951) fifty-seven times in succession. He was given his very own copy of the movie as a reward.

Dennis Hopper's *The Last Movie* (1971) has a record thirty minutes of action in it before the opening credits roll.

Sidney Ling was only 13 when he directed *Les the Wonderdog* (1972). He also produced the film and wrote the script.

The longest commercial movie of all time is the German *Die Zweite Heimat*. It was directed by Edgar Reitz and it runs for over twenty-five hours. (Reitz's earlier *Heimat* is a mere fifteen and a half hours by comparison.)

The longest movie ever made is *The Cure for Insomnia* (1987) by John Henry Timmins. Premièred in Chicago, it runs for eighty-five hours, though a ridiculously short eighty-hour version is also available for those who fear they may nod off with the full enchilada.

The longest Oscar speech on record is Greer Garson's five-and-a-half-minute effort in 1942 after she won for *Mrs. Miniver*.

The most overused line of dialogue in films is thought to be "Let's get out of here," which has been used at least once in 81 percent of films, according to statisticians.

The longest time span between a film and its sequel is twenty years: Claude Lelouch's *A Man and a Woman* (1966) and its (imaginatively titled) sequel *A Man and a Woman: Twenty Years Later* (1986).

The shortest dialogue script for a movie is one word in Mel Brooks' *Silent Movie* (1976)—spoken, appropriately enough, by mime artist Marcel Marceau. The word is "Non."

The soft-porn movie *Emmanuelle* (1974) ran for no fewer than ten years and eight months in Paris, from its release until February 1985.

Director Michael Cimino shot 1.5 million feet of film for *Heaven's Gate* (1980). If the movie was shown unedited, it would have run for over nine days.

The largest cast ever assembled for a movie was 187,000 for the German Napoleonic epic *Kolberg* (1944). (The cast vastly exceeded the number of people who actually went to see the film.)

ROLE–PLAY
20 stars who went beyond the call of duty for their roles

WARREN BEATTY
During one scene in *Bonnie and Clyde* (1967), which he produced, he ordered a peach from another state to be flown onto the movie lot, because they were out of season in Texas, where they were shooting.

MARTIN SHEEN
Stayed drunk for two days for a drunk scene in *Apocalypse Now* (1979). (Maybe that explains why the blood in the broken mirror scene is actually his own.)

DANIEL DAY-LEWIS
For *The Last of the Mohicans* (1992), he went to a survival camp in Alabama and learned how to live off the land by tracking animals and generally living by his wits.

AL PACINO
While researching the part of a policeman in *Serpico* (1973), he made a citizen's arrest.

DUSTIN HOFFMAN
After he had stayed up all night to look tired for a scene in *Marathon Man* (1976), his costar Laurence Olivier commented, "Why don't you try acting, my good man?"

BRAD PITT
Had one of his front teeth chipped and shaved his head to look suitably menacing for *The Fight Club* (1999).

GLENN CLOSE

Consulted three psychoanalysts during the making of *Fatal Attraction* (1987) in order to try to understand the psychosis of the character she was playing.

JON VOIGHT

Spent five weeks learning to play basketball from a wheelchair for *Coming Home* (1978).

NICOLAS CAGE

Had two teeth yanked out without an anesthetic to look more authentic as a vampire in *Vampire's Kiss* (1989). (He also ate six live cockroaches in this film.)

MONTGOMERY CLIFT

Spent a night locked up on Death Row in the San Quentin Penitentiary to prepare for the final scene in *A Place in the Sun* (1951), where he's sentenced to death.

MERYL STREEP

For *Sophie's Choice* (1982), not only did she learn to speak both German and Polish fluently, but she also shaved her head and lost 25 pounds for the Auschwitz scenes.

ROD STEIGER

When Julie Christie slapped him in a scene in *Dr. Zhivago* (1965), he instinctively hit her back. David Lean left the altercation in the scene, even though it wasn't in the script.

GENE HACKMAN

Spent two weeks in a patrol car doing the rounds with a real detective in order to get into the mood for playing Popeye Doyle in *The French Connection* (1971).

JANE WYMAN

To get into the mind of a deaf mute for *Johnny Belinda* (1948), she studied signing and lip reading with experts, worked with the handicapped to familiarize herself with their daily routines, and wore plastic earplugs on the set to blot out external sounds.

BEN KINGSLEY
To play Gandhi in the movie of that name, he went on a vegetarian diet, lost 17 pounds, went bald, took up yoga, and even learned how to spin thread.

JAMES CAAN
Spent so much time with gangland hoods when researching the part of Sonny Corleone in *The Godfather* (1972) that at one point he was almost arrested by the FBI.

JACK LEMMON
To prepare himself for his coruscating role in *Days of Wine and Roses* (1962), he attended AA meetings, went to hospitals to watch alcoholics drying out, and got so immersed in the straitjacket scene of the movie that director Blake Edwards had to shake him quiet even after the cameras stopped rolling.

FAYE DUNAWAY
Lost 20 pounds to look suitably gaunt for *Bonnie and Clyde* (1967) by hauling sandbags about the place.

WARREN BEATTY
Learned Russian to prepare for the role of John Reed in *Reds* (1981).

ROBERT DUVALL
Actually got a job singing in a C&W bar to prepare himself for his Oscar-winning role as a country singer in Bruce Beresford's *Tender Mercies* (1983). (He also wrote eight of the songs that featured in the final print of the movie.)

THE ROAD NOT TAKEN

20 lead-role refusals that may surprise you (the actors who turned down the role, the film, and the actors who finally took the role)

Montgomery Clift (*Sunset Boulevard*, 1950) William Holden
Kirk Douglas (*Cat Ballou*, 1965) Lee Marvin
W. C. Fields (*The Wizard of Oz*, 1939) Frank Morgan
Jane Fonda (*Bonnie and Clyde*, 1967) Faye Dunaway
William Holden (*The Guns of Navarone*, 1961) Gregory Peck
Alan Ladd (*Giant*, 1956) James Dean
Hedy Lamarr (*Casablanca*, 1942) Ingrid Bergman
Burt Lancaster (*Ben Hur*, 1959) Charlton Heston
George Raft (*Casablanca*, 1942) Humphrey Bogart
Laurence Olivier (*Judgment at Nuremberg*, 1966) Spencer Tracy
Laurence Harvey (*Alfie*, 1966) Michael Caine
Albert Finney (*Lawrence of Arabia*, 1962) Peter O'Toole
James Mason (*Who's Afraid of Virginia Woolf?*, 1966) Richard Burton
Cary Grant (*My Fair Lady,* 1964) Rex Harrison
Gregory Peck (*High Noon*, 1952) Gary Cooper
Greta Garbo (*The Country Girl*, 1954) Grace Kelly
James Mason (*The King and I*, 1956) Yul Brynner
David Niven (*The African Queen*, 1951) Humphrey Bogart
Bette Davis (*Who's Afraid of Virginia Woolf?*,1966) Elizabeth Taylor
Mae West (*Sunset Boulevard*, 1950) Gloria Swanson

5 ROLE REFUSALS THAT MADE STARS OF THE SECOND CHOICES

Dustin Hoffman in *The Graduate* (1967). Became a star overnight after Robert Redford refused the role.

Warren Beatty refused both parts in *Butch Cassidy and the Sundance Kid* (1969). The film became a milestone for Paul Newman, and gave Robert Redford the leg up that he needed onto Hollywood's A-list ladder. (Marlon Brando also refused the Redford role.)

Frank Sinatra in *The Man with The Golden Arm* (1955). Brando said no and the role revived Sinatra's flagging career.

Shirley Temple was originally supposed to appear in *The Wizard of Oz* (1939) but couldn't be released from her studio for contractual reasons, which was why Judy Garland got the part.

Debra Winger turned down the role that made Glenn Close a star in *Fatal Attraction* (1987).

NO, NO, A THOUSAND TIMES NO
5 multiple refusals

Robert Redford can cry into his beer after pooh-poohing this lot: *The Graduate, Rosemary's Baby, Love Story, The Day of the Jackal, Who's Afraid of Virginia Woolf?,* and *The Verdict*.

Warren Beatty balked at three movies that became star vehicles for Robert Redford: *The Way We Were, The Sting,* and *The Great Gatsby.*

Sigourney Weaver had first option on three steamy potboilers: *Fatal Attraction, Body Heat,* and *9½ Weeks.*

Jack Nicholson has managed to stay as one of Hollywood's most bankable stars over three decades, despite refusing lead roles in movies such as *The Untouchables, The China Syndrome, Apocalypse Now, Coming Home, The Great Gatsby, The Sting,* and *The Godfather.* Asked why he refused the Michael Corleone role in the latter, he said rather strangely: "I thought you had to be Jewish to play him."

Not only did George Raft refuse three vehicles that became hits for Humphrey Bogart (*Casablanca, High Sierra* and *The Maltese Falcon*), but also the classic Billy Wilder thriller *Double Indemnity.*

WHY I SAID NO
10 stars' reasons for refusing a part

MARLON BRANDO
Had been inked in to play the role that eventually went to Kirk Douglas in Elia Kazan's *The Arrangement* (1969). He pulled out when Martin Luther King was assassinated, informing Kazan that he was thinking of retiring from movies altogether to devote himself to social issues.

R

MONTGOMERY CLIFT
Refused the William Holden part in *Sunset Boulevard* (1950)
because he felt that the idea of a man living with an older
woman in a semi-gigolo-like relationship would hurt his image.
(Ironically, this was very close to his real-life situation with
Libby Holman.)

JACK NICHOLSON
Said no to the Martin Sheen role in *Apocalypse Now* (1979)
because it would have necessitated spending six months in the
Philippine jungle.

ROBERT REDFORD
Balked at the role in *The Verdict* (1982) for which Paul Newman
received an Oscar nomination because the character was too old
for him. (In other words, his own age!)

ROBERT DE NIRO
Considered playing Jesus in *The Last Temptation of Christ*
(1988) but turned it down finally, feeling that his concentration
would have been diverted by all the actors who had done the
part before.

ELVIS PRESLEY
Was tempted to play the Kris Kristofferson role in the remake of
A Star is Born (1976) to revive his (brain-)dead movie career but
ultimately decided that the idea of playing a drug-addicted rock
star was just that bit too near the truth.

SHARON STONE
Said no to the chance of playing opposite Clint Eastwood in *In
The Line of Fire* (1993) because she thought that old Clint was
getting past his prime. The movie proved to be a huge hit for
him and made a star of Rene Russo.

MICHAEL CAINE
Rejected *Women in Love* (1970) because he didn't like the idea of wrestling naked with Alan Bates. Bates wasn't offended and Oliver Reed (a somewhat less inhibited person) stepped in to do the honors.

RICHARD DREYFUSS
Refused the lead role in *All That Jazz* (1979) because he didn't have enough confidence in Bob Fosse as a director. The role won star status for Roy Scheider—and an Oscar nomination as well.

SYLVESTER STALLONE
Pulled out of *Beverly Hills Cop* (1984) because he felt that there weren't enough action scenes in it!

A FAMILY AFFAIR
15 star relations

GERALDINE CHAPLIN
Granddaughter of playwright Eugene O'Neill

OLIVER REED
Nephew of director Carol Reed

PETER LAWFORD
Brother-in-law of John F. Kennedy

SHIRLEY MACLAINE
Sister of Warren Beatty

OLIVIA DE HAVILLAND
Sister of Joan Fontaine

NICOLAS CAGE
Nephew of Francis Ford Coppola

RITA HAYWORTH
First cousin of Ginger Rogers

SOPHIA LOREN
Sister-in-law of Mussolini's son

ANTHONY QUINN
Son-in-law of Cecil B. De Mille

LARRY HAGMAN
Son of musical comedy star Mary Martin

DREW BARRYMORE
Granddaughter of the legendary John

GRIFFIN O'NEAL
Son of Ryan and brother of Tatum

JASON PATRIC
The grandson of Jackie Gleason

MELANIE GRIFFITH
Daughter of Tippi Hedren

MIA FARROW
Daughter of Maureen O'Sullivan

THE POSTMAN ALWAYS RINGS TWICE

15 remakes that used different titles
(originals in brackets)

A Perfect Murder, 1998 (*Dial M. for Murder*, 1954)
Anna and the King, 1999 (*The King and I*, 1956)
Stage Struck, 1958 (*Morning Glory*, 1933)
Stolen Hours, 1963 (*Dark Victory*, 1939)
Silk Stockings, 1957 (*Ninotchka*, 1939)
Switching Channels, 1988 (*The Front Page*, 1974)
Thieves Like Us, 1974 (*They Live by Night*, 1949)
Behind the High Wall, 1956 (*The Big Guy*, 1939)
The Girl Who Had Everything, 1953 (*A Free Soul*, 1931)
Heaven Can Wait, 1978 (*Here Comes Mr. Jordan*, 1941)
The Maltese Falcon, 1941 (*Satan Met a Lady*, 1935)
Cabaret, 1972 (*I Am a Camera*, 1955)
Colorado Territory, 1949 (*High Sierra*, 1941)
You've Got Mail, 1999 (*The Shop Around the Corner*, 1940)
The Rains of Ranchipur, 1955 (*The Rains Came*, 1939)

REPEAT PERFORMANCE

10 pairs of stars who played opposite each other
repeatedly

Jeanette MacDonald and Nelson Eddy (8 times)
Olivia de Havilland and Errol Flynn (8 times)
Katharine Hepburn and Spencer Tracy (10 times)
Ginger Rogers and Fred Astaire (10 times)

Judy Garland and Mickey Rooney (10 times)
Paul Newman and Joanne Woodward (11 times)
Sophia Loren and Marcello Mastroianni (12 times)
Janet Gaynor and Charles Farrell (12 times)
Myrna Loy and William Powell (13 times)
Charles Bronson and Jill Ireland (15 times)

(But the overall prize goes to Indian stars Prem Nazir and Sheela, who played opposite each other no fewer than 130 times in all.)

ONCE MORE WITH FEELING
10 notable retakes

Desire Me (1947)
Robert Mitchum said after making this, "I stopped believing in movies after it took Greer Garson 125 takes to say 'No'."

Some Like It Hot (1959)
It took Marilyn Monroe 41 takes before she could say, "It's me, Sugar," to Billy Wilder's satisfaction. (By this stage Tony Curtis had nibbled forty-one chicken bones.)

The Blue Angel (1930)
Josef von Sternberg shot Marlene Dietrich singing, "Falling in Love Again" 236 times because she couldn't pronounce the word "moths" to his satisfaction. (The way she said it, it sounded like "moss".)

The Shining (1979)
Stanley Kubrick shot one scene with Shelley Duvall 127 times.

Hook (1991)
The special effects team shot a scene thirty times to try to get a leaf to fall through a window onto Caroline Goodall's shoulder. Steven Spielberg then took over. Fifty-one takes later, Spielberg managed the feat…with a fishing pole.

From Hell to Texas (1958)
Henry Hathaway made Dennis Hopper do a scene eighty-five times.

Dr. Strangelove (1964)
Sterling Hayden fluffed a take for one scene forty-seven times.

City Lights (1931)
Charlie Chaplin ordered a record 342 retakes of the scene where a blind girl sells him a flower, imagining that he is a rich tycoon.

The Electric Horseman (1979)
One particular take was shot forty-eight times. (That's 7,500 feet of film—for what became a twenty-second sequence.)

The Scarlet Letter (1995)
Demi Moore ordered a scene to be reshot at a cost of $100,000 because she didn't like the way her hair looked in it.

HITTING PAY DIRT
20 interesting salaries

MICHAEL CAINE
Did *Mona Lisa* (1986) for his friend Bob Hoskins for "two bob and a lollipop."

MARILYN MONROE
Received $50 for her famous nude calendar shot. It eventually netted the calendar company in excess of $750,000.

TREVOR HOWARD
His most famous role, that in *Brief Encounter* (1945), was worth no more than £500 to him.

ROBERT DE NIRO
He received $50 for his first screen role, in *The Wedding Party* (1969). Compare that to the $1.5 million he received for eleven days on the set of *The Untouchables* (1987).

MARLON BRANDO
Earned $4 million for three days' work on *Superman* (1978).

SYLVESTER STALLONE
For the movie *The Lords of Flatbush* (1974), he said that he received just twenty-five free T-shirts.

BOB HOSKINS
Received $200,000 from Francis Ford Coppola for agreeing to play Al Capone in *The Untouchables* (1987) if Robert de Niro wasn't available. He said to Coppola after the windfall, "If there's any other parts you don't want me to play, let me know."

KIM BASINGER
Turned down $5 million to appear in a sequel to *9½ Weeks*.

ROBERT MITCHUM
Appeared in seven Hopalong Cassidy films at the beginning of his career for "$100 a week plus all the horse manure I could take home."

SIGOURNEY WEAVER
Her $18 million for *Alien 5* (1999) set a new record for women's salaries.

ELIZABETH TAYLOR
The first female star to command $1 million for a performance (in *Cleopatra*, 1963).

JODIE FOSTER
Received $15 million for *Anna and the King* (1999).

TOM CRUISE
Pocketed $20 million for *Jerry Maguire* (1996).

EDDIE MURPHY
Was offered $20 million for *The Nutty Professor 2* (1999).

HARRISON FORD
Earned $20 million for *Air Force One* (1997).

JIM CARREY
Received $17 million for *The Cable Guy* (1996).

CARY GRANT
Donated his (then astronomical) $125,000 salary for *The Philadelphia Story* (1940) to the British War Relief Fund.

LAURENCE HARVEY
Performed in *Darling* (1965) without demanding a fee: he hoped that it would act as a window of opportunity for him.

WILLIAM HURT
Did his Oscar-winning role in *Kiss of the Spider Woman* (1985) for nothing (as did most of the cast), when the production was threatened with being shut down due to lack of finance.

MARTIN SHEEN
Donated his fee for *Gandhi* (1982) to charity.

SCHOOL'S OUT
5 high–school experiences

ELVIS PRESLEY
When he was in the eighth grade, his music teacher said that he showed no promise as a singer.

MARLON BRANDO
Used to wander so much on his way to kindergarten that his sister Jocelyn eventually had to bring him on a leash.

JACK NICHOLSON
Was once kept in detention every day for a whole school year.

ERROL FLYNN
Expelled from three schools for stealing; and a fourth, for making love to a girl in a coal-heap.

TOM CRUISE
Voted "Least Likely to Succeed" in high school.

ME, MYSELF, AND I

20 actors who played themselves on screen

Orson Welles (*Follow the Boys*, 1944)
Johnny Weissmuller (*Stage Door Canteen*, 1943)
Humphrey Bogart (*The Love Lottery*, 1954)
Gary Cooper (*Variety Girl*, 1947)
Elliott Gould (*Nashville*, 1975)
Lionel Barrymore (*Free and Easy*, 1930)
Tommy Steele (*Kill Me Tomorrow*, 1957)
Bob Hope (*The Oscar*, 1966)
Gene Kelly (*Love is Better Than Ever*, 1962)
Jackie Coogan (*Free and Easy*, 1930)
Buster Keaton (*Sunset Boulevard*, 1950)
Cary Grant (*Without Reservations*, 1946)
Sean Connery (*Memories of Me*, 1988)
W. C. Fields (*Never Give a Sucker an Even Break*, 1941)
Frank Sinatra (*Cannonball Run II*, 1983)
Edward G. Robinson (*It's a Great Feeling*, 1949)
Tony Randall (*King of Comedy*, 1983)
Paul Newman (*Silent Movie*, 1976)
Charlie Chaplin (*Show People*, 1928)
Ronald Reagan (*It's a Great Feeling*, 1949)

S

10 ACTRESSES WHO PLAYED THEMSELVES ON SCREEN

Marlene Dietrich (*Follow the Boys*, 1944)
Liza Minnelli (*The Muppets Take Manhattan*, 1984)
Greta Garbo (*A Man's Man*)
Joan Crawford (*It's a Great Feeling*, 1949)
Anne Bancroft (*Silent Movie*, 1976)
Katharine Hepburn (*Stage Door Canteen*, 1943)
Julie Christie (*Nashville*, 1975)
Natalie Wood (*The Candidate*, 1972)
Brigitte Bardot (*Dear Brigitte*, 1965)
Barbara Stanwyck (*Hollywood Canteen*, 1944)

20 STARS WHO PLAYED THEMSELVES IN ROBERT ALTMAN'S 'THE PLAYER' (1992)

Louise Fletcher	Burt Reynolds
Teri Garr	Julia Roberts
Jeff Goldblum	Susan Sarandon
Elliott Gould	Natalie Wood
Anjelica Huston	Bruce Willis
Sally Kellerman	Lily Tomlin
Sally Kirkland	Rod Steiger
Jack Lemmon	Cher
Marlee Matlin	Karen Black
Nick Nolte	James Coburn

EVERYTHING YOU EVER WANTED TO KNOW ...
15 sex-related movie facts

1897
Le Bain de la Parisienne brings nudity to the screen for the first time in the eponymous city.

1910
Denmark releases the very first full-length sex picture, *The White Slave Traffic*.

1913
America makes its first feature-length sex movie, *Traffic in Souls*.

1934
The Hays Code clamps down on suggestive material in films, thus making Hollywood sex covert rather than overt for the next thirty (very) odd years.

1951
The Swedish movie *One Summer of Happiness*, featuring nude scenes, is passed by the British Board of Film Censors.

1961
This year sees the release of *Victim*, the first British motion picture to deal frankly with homosexuality.

1966
Britain's first group-sex scene occurs in Antonioni's *Blow-Up*.

1968
Susannah York indulges in a spot of lesbian seduction in *The Killing of Sister George*.

1969
Alan Bates and Oliver Reed romp around in the nude in the screen adaptation of D. H. Lawrence's *Women in Love*.

1972
Marlon Brando finds a new use for butter as he bangs Maria Schneider in *Last Tango in Paris*.

1981
Lots of huffing and puffing between Jack Nicholson and Jessica Lange on a kitchen table in Bob Rafelson's grim depression parable, *The Postman Always Rings Twice*.

1985
More designer angst, with Mickey Rourke humping a delectable Kim Basinger on a coffee table—among other places—in *$9^{1}/_{2}$ Weeks*.

1987
Michael Douglas and Glenn Close rattle the dishes in the sink as they get close and personal in Adrian Lyne's trendsetting chiller *Fatal Attraction*.

1992
Lesbian serial killer Sharon Stone gives new meaning to the term "He came and then he went," as she shows lovers a much better use for ice picks in *Basic Instinct*.

1997
Jeremy Irons sets tongues wagging about the alleged romanti-cization of pedophilia in Adrian Lyne's remake of *Lolita,* in which he falls head over heels in love with the delectable (but oh-so-young) Dominique Swain.

WE'RE NO ANGELS
5 sex–kitten roles that broke actresses into the bigtime

BO DEREK in *10* (1979)
A cornrow hairstyle, legs up to her shoulders, face to die for…
and making out with cuddly Dudley Moore to Ravel's "Bolero."

RAQUEL WELCH in *One Million Years B.C.* (1966)
The cast only emit primeval grunts when lovely Raquel appears
in the designer-shag cavewoman bikini, which may or may not
be a form of prehistoric mating call.

URSULA ANDRESS in *Dr. No* (1962)
The phenomenon of Ms. Undress (sorry, Andress) on a beach in
that get-up is something that not even Q could have prepared
James Bond for.

JANE FONDA in *Barbarella* (1968)
Who would ever have thought that this futuristic bimboesque
creature would turn into an antiwar propagandist and social cru-
sader?

SHARON STONE in *Basic Instinct* (1992)
After a decade knocking on the Hollywood door in innumerable
forgettable romps, Sharon hit pay dirt big time as a bisexual novel-
ist who takes the term "killing off your characters" quite literally.

CRIMES AND MISDEMEANORS
10 celebrities who were involved in sex scandals

WOODY ALLEN
Brought all kinds of problems on himself when his long-term
partner Mia Farrow found nude photographs of Soon-Yi (the
daughter she adopted with her former husband André Previn) in
a drawer in Allen's apartment. He went on to marry her and Mia
proved hell hath no fury like a woman scorned when she
accused him of all manner of sexual abuse, the final judicial
decision severely limiting the amount of time he was allowed to
spend with his children.

ERROL FLYNN
Charged with double statutory rape in 1942. Having had a
history of bedding nymphets and raping a previous wife, his
acquittal was near-miraculous, but the two ladies involved turned
out to have checkered sexual histories as well.

HUGH GRANT
Did the bad thing with hooker Divine Brown when he kerb-
crawled, dropped his pants, sought some oral gratification, and
got caught, thus breaking the Eleventh Commandment for
movie stars.

JACK NICHOLSON
Taken to court in 1997 by two prostitutes, whom he refused to
pay for their favors.

CHARLIE CHAPLIN
Had a lifelong passion for deflowering underage maidens, which
sometimes got him into court.

S

CHARLIE SHEEN

When Madam Queen Heidi Fleiss' little (or maybe big) red book finally hit the world's stage, Charlie's name was in it in big bold letters. He was said to have spent up to $2,000 per week being entertained by her—and he still thought he was getting a bargain.

MICHAEL DOUGLAS

A self-declared sexaholic who actually went into therapy to get "cured."

ROMAN POLANSKI

Arrested in 1977 on suspicion for having drugged and then raped a 13-year-old girl in Jack Nicholson's house. He was found guilty of having sex with a minor, but was allowed bail in order to shoot a movie called *Hurricane in Tahiti*. He neither made the picture nor returned to the States, where he still remains a fugitive from justice.

JEAN HARLOW

Her husband Paul Bern shot himself just two months into their marriage, reputedly because she maligned his ability to "perform" in the boudoir.

JOAN CRAWFORD

Alleged to have made a string of sex films in the 1920s and persuaded MGM to try to buy them up and destroy them. When one possessor of some nude shots refused to part with them, his house was burned down three weeks later, himself being a casualty as well as the pictures.

NO SEX, PLEASE, WE'RE THESPIANS
5 stars who might need some Viagra

BURT REYNOLDS
His main problem at the peak of his womanizing, he said, was what to do with big tits after ten minutes.

RICHARD HARRIS
He believed sex ruins marriage.

ARNOLD SCHWARZENNEGER
"Many times while I was getting laid," he said once, "in my head I was doing a business deal."

MICKEY ROURKE
Once said that he preferred motorbikes to sex.

SHIRLEY MACLAINE
Claims that people are generally happier when sex becomes a non-issue in their lives.

SEX, LIES, AND VIDEOTAPE
10 stars' reactions to movie sex

"After a couple of days doing love scenes, I just want to hop back into my trousers again." (Matt Dillon)

"Making love on the screen is the most sexless and boring thing in the whole world." (Joan Collins)

"When I'm trying to play serious love scenes with her, she's positioning her bottom for the best angle shots."
(Stephen Boyd on Brigitte Bardot)

"I've become the greatest at screen orgasms. Ten seconds of heavy breathing, roll your head from side to side, simulate a slight asthma attack...and die a little." (Candice Bergen)

"Darling, if I get excited during this scene, please forgive me. And if I *don't* get excited, please forgive me."
(Tom Berenger to a costar during a movie romp)

"It's not that difficult to lie around naked on top of Debbie Harry all day. You know what I mean?" (James Woods)

"It's like dance steps, or a fight scene. When she scratches your back, you have to arch two beats, then roll over, boom."
(Michael Douglas)

"I usually end up sobbing in the dressing room after every take."
(Kathleen Turner)

"It's kind of hard playing a whore when you're walking round with a sheet pasted to your breasts like Doris Day."
(Brooke Shields after going flat-chested to play a character younger than herself in *Pretty Baby*)

"You say things you never thought of to a girl you've met only a few days before, surrounded by people you don't know."
(Marcello Mastroianni)

SING FOR YOUR SUPPER
20 nonsingers in singing roles

Audrey Hepburn (*Breakfast at Tiffany's*, 1961)

Marlon Brando (*Guys and Dolls*, 1955)

Sissy Spacek (*Coal Miner's Daughter*, 1980)

Meryl Streep (*Postcards from the Edge*, 1991)

Lee Marvin (*Paint Your Wagon*, 1969)

Clint Eastwood (*Paint Your Wagon*, 1969)

Woody Allen (*Everyone Says I Love You*, 1996)

Robert de Niro (*New York, New York*, 1977)

Richard Attenborough (*Dr. Doolittle*, 1967)

Sean Connery (*Darby O'Gill and the Little People*, 1959)

Jack Nicholson (*Heartburn*, 1986)

Natalie Wood (*West Side Story*, 1961)

Rod Steiger (*Oklahoma*, 1955)

Rex Harrison (*My Fair Lady*, 1964)

Mel Brooks (*High Anxiety*, 1977)

Mitzi Gaynor (*South Pacific*, 1958)

Harry Dean Stanton (*Renaldo and Clara*, 1978)

Gary Busey (*The Buddy Holly Story*, 1978)

Demi Moore (*No Small Affair*, 1984)

Michelle Pfeiffer (*The Fabulous Baker Boys*, 1989)

THANK YOU FOR THE MUSIC
25 songs made famous by the movies

I Could Have Danced All Night
(*My Fair Lady*, 1964)

Raindrops Keep Fallin' on My Head
(*Butch Cassidy and the Sundance Kid*, 1969)

Well Did You Ever
(*High Society*, 1956)

Everybody's Talking
(*Midnight Cowboy*, 1969)

Moon River
(*Breakfast at Tiffany's*, 1961)

High Hopes
(*A Hole in the Head*, 1959)

Windmills of Your Mind
(*The Thomas Crown Affair*, 1968)

I Was Born Under a Wanderin' Star
(*Paint Your Wagon*, 1970)

Que Sera Sera
(*The Man Who Knew Too Much*, 1956)

Secret Love
(*Calamity Jane*, 1953)

Zip-a-Dee-Doo-Dah
(*Song of the South*, 1946)

Have Yourself a Merry Little Christmas
(*Meet Me in St. Louis*, 1944)

White Christmas
(*Holiday Inn*, 1942)

Over the Rainbow
(*The Wizard of Oz*, 1939)

I'm Gonna Wash That Man Right Outta My Hair
(*South Pacific*, 1958)

Up Where We Belong
(*An Officer and a Gentleman*, 1982)

I Had the Time of My Life
(*Dirty Dancing*, 1987)

Mrs. Robinson
(*The Graduate*, 1967)

You're the One That I Want
(*Grease*, 1978)

Night Fever
(*Saturday Night Fever*, 1977)

You'll Never Walk Alone
(*Carousel*, 1956)

Unchained Melody
(*Ghost*, 1990)

Bright Eyes
(*Watership Down*, 1987)

The Lady is a Tramp
(*Pal Joey*, 1957)

Let's Face the Music
(*Follow the Fleet*, 1936)

BE A SPORT
10 sports stars who've played themselves

O. J. Simpson (*The Klansman*, 1974)
Babe Ruth (*Pride of the Yankees*, 1942)
John McEnroe (*Players*, 1979)
Muhammad Ali (*The Greatest*, 1977)
Bjorn Borg (*Racquet*, 1979)
Floyd Patterson (*Terrible Joe Moran,* 1984)
Arnold Palmer (*Call Me Bwana*, 1963)
Joe Frazier (*Rocky*, 1977)
Ilie Nastase (*Players*, 1979)
Stirling Moss (*The Beauty Contest*, 1964)

SHOOTING STARS
10 stars who committed suicide

CAROLE LANDIS
Took an overdose when she realized that Rex Harrison was never going to leave his wife Lilli Palmer for her.

PIER ANGELI
A deeply troubled woman whose marriage to Vic Damone was a disaster, she said love died for her the day James Dean (the man whose proposal of marriage she rejected) was killed in a car crash.

PEG ENTWISTLE
This wannabe actress finally realized that she wasn't going to make it in Tinseltown's rat race and hurled herself to her death from the thirteenth letter of Beverly Hills' HOLLYWOOD-LAND sign. The "LAND" part of the sign was later removed.

JEAN SEBERG
She was chosen from 80,000 hopefuls by Otto Preminger to play the title role in *Joan of Arc* (1957), but her success was short-lived. After she took up the cause of the Black Panthers, she was dogged almost to the death by the FBI. Amid rumors that she was having an affair with one of them she went to a car park with a bottle of pills at the age of 41.

ALBERT DEKKER
Hanged himself in 1968 in his Hollywood home. He was dressed in women's silk underwear when found, and his suicide note was written on his own body. In lipstick.

MARGAUX HEMINGWAY
Like Papa Hemingway, her grandpapa, did a hara-kiri in 1997 when her career failed to take off like that of her sister Mariel.

She was also an epileptic and had a drinking problem.

PINA PELLICER
One of the many former lovers of Marlon Brando (her one moment of screen glory was acting opposite him in *One-Eyed Jacks*, 1961), who developed psychological problems after their brief fling ended. She committed suicide just before Christmas in 1964.

JOHN GILBERT
Drank himself to death after his (then) wife Marlene Dietrich had an affair with Gary Cooper in 1936.

DIANE BARRYMORE
This daughter of John Barrymore did herself in when she was just 39. A chronic alcoholic, the title of her autobiography says it all: *Too Much Too Soon*.

ALAN LADD
Killed himself with a lethal cocktail of booze and tranquilizers in 1964. Some people have speculated that the overdose may have been accidental, but he was suffering from depression. Strangely, as a boy he unwittingly gave his mother money to buy the ant powder with which she also topped herself.

THANK YOUR LUCKY STARS
5 superstitious performers

LEONARD NIMOY
Wears an old woolen hat whenever he tries out for a new part because he wore it for the original audition of *Star Trek*.

 Zsa Zsa Gabor
Believes that if you break a mirror you'll have bad luck for the
rest of your life, unless you go to Paris, stand on the Pont
Alexandre III, and throw the pieces over your shoulder into the
Seine.

John Wayne
If he was playing poker and a card turned face up by accident,
he made its owner stand up and circle the table three times.

Liza Minnelli
Never travels without a pair of old red slippers.

Elizabeth Taylor
Always insisted that her dressing rooms were painted violet.

FAREWELL, MY LOVELY
15 notable swan–song performances

Humphrey Bogart (*The Harder They Fall*, 1956)
Grace Kelly (*High Society*, 1956)
James Dean (*Giant*, 1956)
Tyrone Power (*Witness for the Prosecution*, 1957)
Clark Gable (*The Misfits*, 1961)
Marilyn Monroe (*The Misfits*, 1961)
Alan Ladd (*The Carpetbaggers*, 1964)
Ronald Reagan (*The Killers*, 1964)
Spencer Tracy (*Guess Who's Coming to Dinner*, 1967)
Peter Finch (*Network*, 1976)
John Wayne (*The Shootist*, 1976)
Steve McQueen (*The Hunter*, 1980)

Henry Fonda (*On Golden Pond*, 1981)
Pat O'Brien (*Ragtime*, 1981)
Burt Lancaster (*Field of Dreams*, 1989)

TAYLOR-MADE FOR MARRIAGE
10 quotes from Liz Taylor on marital bliss

"Your heart knows when you meet the right man. There is no doubt that Nicky is the one I want to spend my life with."
(After her marriage to Nicky Hilton in 1950.)

"I just want to be with Michael. This, for me, is the beginning of a happy end."
(After she divorced Hilton to marry Michael Wilding in 1952.)

"This marriage will last for ever. For me it will be third time lucky."
(Her ominous prophecy after divorcing Wilding to marry Mike Todd in 1957. Shortly afterwards, he died in a plane crash.)

"I have never been happier in my life. We will be on our honeymoon for thirty or forty years."
(After marriage to Eddie Fisher in 1959.)

"I'm so happy you can't believe it. I love him enough to stand by him no matter what he might do."
(After her marriage to Richard Burton in 1964.)

"There will be bloody no more marriages or divorces. We're stuck like chicken feathers to tar—for always."
(After her second marriage to Burton in 1975.)

"I don't think of John as Husband Number Seven. He's Number One all the way—the best lover I've ever had. I want to spend the rest of my life with him and I want to be buried with him." (Following her seventh wedding, this time to John Warner in 1976.)

"I only sleep with men I've been married to. How many other women can make that claim?"
(When she was accused of being promiscuous.)

"What's this—a memory test?"
(In tetchy mood with the registrar after the Warner wedding, when asked to name her previous husbands.)

"With God's blessing, this is it, forever."
(After her 1991 marriage to Larry Fortensky; with or without God's blessing, however, it wasn't.)

CLASS ACTS
5 stars who were schoolteachers

Gabriel Byrne
George C. Scott
Margaret Hamilton
Ramon Novarro
Sir Michael Redgrave

THE MAGIC RECTANGLE
5 feature films that spawned TV series

Dr. Kildare (1938)
Shane (1953)
M*A*S*H (1970)
The Thin Man (1934)
The Naked City (1948)

FROM THE SMALL SCREEN TO THE SILVER ONE
15 TV series that became movies

The X-Files (1998)
The Addams Family (1991)
Batman (1989)
The Flintstones (1994)
The Fugitive (1993)
The Brady Bunch (1995)
The Untouchables (1987)
Mission Impossible (1996)
The Saint (1997)
The Avengers (1998)
Lost in Space (1998)
Dragnet (1987)
Superman (1978)
Star Trek (1979)
The Beverly Hillbillies (1993)

20 ACTORS WHO WENT FROM THE TV SCREEN TO THE BIG SCREEN

Gabriel Byrne (*Bracken*)
Michael Douglas (*The Streets of San Francisco*)
Robin Williams (*Mork and Mindy*)
James Arness *(Gunsmoke)*
Michael J. Fox (*Family Ties*)
Ryan O'Neal (*Peyton Place*)
Danny de Vito (*Taxi*)
Steve McQueen (*Wanted Dead or Alive*)
Jim Carrey (*In Living Color*)
Bruce Willis (*Moonlighting*)
Richard Chamberlain (*Dr. Kildare*)
Phil Silvers *(Sergeant Bilko)*
Nick Nolte (*Rich Man, Poor Man*)
George Clooney (*E.R.*)
Will Smith (*The Fresh Prince of Bel Air*)
David Caruso (*N.Y.P.D. Blue*)
Leonardo DiCaprio (*Growing Pains*)
Brad Pitt (*Dallas*)
Tom Hanks (*Bosom Buddies*)
Woody Harrelson (*Cheers*)

15 ACTRESSES WHO WENT FROM THE TV SCREEN TO THE BIG SCREEN

Kathleen Turner (*The Doctors*)
Sigourney Weaver (*Somerset*)
Sally Field (*Gidget*)

Goldie Hawn (*Rowan and Martin Laugh-In*)

Patty Duke (*The Brighter Day*)

Mia Farrow (*Peyton Place*)

Susan Sarandon (*A World Apart*)

Pamela Anderson (*Baywatch*)

Joan Cusack (*Saturday Night Live*)

Jamie Lee Curtis (*Operation Petticoat*)

Neve Campbell (*Party of Five*)

Meg Ryan (*As the World Turns*)

Demi Moore (*General Hospital*)

Shelley Long (*Cheers*)

Catherine Zeta Jones (*The Darling Buds of May*)

I *AM* BIG, IT'S THE PICTURES THAT GOT SMALL

20 stars who found a niche on the TV screen after the big one

Bill Cosby (*The Cosby Show*)

Larry Hagman (*Dallas*)

Joan Collins (*Dynasty*)

David Janssen (*The Fugitive*)

John Lithgow (*Third Rock from the Sun*)

Jack Lord (*Hawaii Five-O*)

Lucille Ball (*I Love Lucy*)

Peter Falk (*Columbo*)

Candice Bergen (*Murphy Brown*)

Jane Wyman (*Falcon Crest*)

Raymond Burr (*Ironside*)
Lee J. Cobb (*The Virginian*)
John Forsyth (*Dynasty*)
Telly Savalas (*Kojak*)
James Garner (*The Rockford Files*)
Charlton Heston (*The Colbys*)
David McCallum (*The Man from U.N.C.L.E.*)
Karl Malden (*The Streets of San Francisco*)
Burt Reynolds (*Evening Shade*)
Tony Curtis (*The Persuaders*)

ALTERED STATES
15 films whose titles were changed

Whiskey Galore (1949)
This became *Tight Little Island* in the U.S.A. because the Hays
office didn't like the bacchanalian implications of the other title.

Dr. No (1963)
This was rather literally translated in Japan to read *No Need for
a Doctor*.

Not as a Stranger (1955)
Some genius released this in Hong Kong as, wait for it, *The
Heart of a Lady as Pure as a Full Moon Over the Place of
Medical Salvation*.

13 Rue Madeline (1946)
The original number was 32, but director Darryl F. Zanuck
changed it because thirteen was his lucky number.

Sometimes a Great Notion (1971)
This fine title, adapted from Ken Kesey's novel of the same name, became bowdlerized into the more catchy *Never Give an Inch* for its TV run.

The Sun Also Rises (1957)
It was felt that Ernest Hemingway's original title, *Fiesta*, would conjure up too many exotic overtones.

Burn (1970)
This Marlon Brando movie (his favorite) was originally titled *Quiemada*, but it was changed to the above to make it more palatable to mainstream audiences. The name change didn't help and the movie flopped anyway.

Annie Hall (1977)
The original title was *Anhedonia*, which means "a chronic inability to experience pleasure," a condition that Woody Allen claims to suffer from.

The Great Dictator (1940)
The adjective was reluctantly added by Charlie Chaplin for this satire of Adolf Hitler after Paramount informed him that his original title, *The Dictator*, was copyrighted by them from a different work, and would cost him $25,000 to use.

The Devil Takes a Count (1936)
The American title was *The Devil is a Sissy*. It was changed because at the time "sissy" was a British euphemism for homosexual.

Striptease Lady (1943)
Based on Gypsy Rose Lee's novel, *The G-String Murders*, but refused that title because when released, the term "G-string" hadn't passed into common parlance. (It was called *Lady of Burlesque* in the U.S.A.)

The Pope Must Die (1991)
Some American distributors took the title of this gentle comedy literally and refused to touch it until Robbie Coltrane, following the example of some graffiti artists in the British subway, changed it to the decidedly more innocuous *The Pope Must Diet.*

White Men Can't Jump (1992)
The fact that this basketball comedy was released in Italy as *White Men Can't Stick It In* may say all we need to know about American market strategists.

Crocodile Dundee (1986)
The first word was apostrophized in American film theaters to prevent audiences from thinking that it was a movie about crocodiles.

Dangerous Liaisons (1988)
This was based on Christopher Hampton's play *Les Liaisons Dangereuses,* but it was wisely translated for public consumption on the basis that movies with foreign titles tend to die at the box office.

THE LONG RIDERS
10 unusually lengthy movie titles

Who is Harry Kellerman and Why is He Saying These Terrible Things About Me? (1971)

The End of the World in Our Usual Bed in a Night Full of Rain (1978)

I Could Never Have Sex with Any Man Who has So Little Regard for My Husband (1973)

Oh Dad, Poor Dad, Mama's Hung You in the Closet and I'm Feelin' So Sad (1967)

Can Hieronymous Merkin Ever Forget Mercy Humppe and Find True Happiness? (1969)

Dr. Strangelove, Or How I Learned to Stop Worrying and Love the Bomb (1963)

Everything You Always Wanted to Know About Sex, But Were Afraid to Ask (1972)

Ja, Ja Mein General! But Which Way to the Front? (1970)

The History of Post-War Japan as Told by a Bar Hostess (1970)

Throw Away Your Books, Let's Go into the Streets (1971)

DOUBLE LIVES
5 British movies that changed their titles for the American market (original titles first)

Home at Seven (Murder on Monday, 1953)
Dark Eyes of London (The Human Monster, 1939)
Night of the Eagle (Burn, Witch, Burn, 1962)
A Matter of Life and Death (If This Be Sin, 1949)
Twinky (Lola, 1971)

5 AMERICAN MOVIES THAT CHANGED THEIR TITLES FOR THE BRITISH MARKET

Never Give a Sucker an Even Break (What a Man, 1941)
Pardon Us (Jailbirds, 1931)
Smash Up (A Woman Destroyed, 1947)
*Those Daring Young Men in their Jaunty Jalopies
(Monte Carlo or Bust*, 1969)
*The Fortune Cookie (Meet Whiplash Willi*e, 1966)

A LINE TO REMEMBER
15 trademark lines from classic movies

"I love the smell of napalm in the morning."
(Robert Duvall, *Apocalypse Now*, 1979)

"We rob banks." (Warren Beatty, *Bonnie and Clyde*, 1967)

"You ain't seen nothin' yet." (Al Jolson, *The Jazz Singer*, 1927)

"You talkin' to me?" (Robert de Niro, *Taxi Driver*, 1977)

"I'll be back." (Arnold Schwarzenegger, *The Terminator*, 1984)

"I coulda bin a contender."
(Marlon Brando, *On the Waterfront*, 1954)

"Frankly, my dear, I don't give a damn."
(Clark Gable, *Gone with the Wind*, 1939)

"Go ahead, punk. Make my day."
(Clint Eastwood, *Sudden Impact*, 1983)

"Phone home." (E.T. in *E.T. The Extra-Terrestrial*, 1982)

"I am big. It's the pictures that got small."
(Gloria Swanson in *Sunset Boulevard*, 1950)

"Mrs. Robinson, you're trying to seduce me, aren't you?"
(Dustin Hoffman in *The Graduate*, 1967)

"Take your stinking paws off me you dirty ape."
(Charlton Heston in *Planet of the Apes*, 1967)

"Life is like a box of chocolates: you never know what you're going to get." (Tom Hanks in *Forrest Gump*, 1994)

"Who are these guys?" (Paul Newman referring to his mysterious pursuers in *Butch Cassidy and the Sundance Kid*, 1969)

"Fasten your seatbelts. It's going to be a bumpy night."
(Bette Davis in *All About Eve*, 1950)

LIFE'S A DRAG
5 Hollywood transvestites

MICHAEL CAINE
Camped it up to play a transvestite killer in Brian de Palma's *Dressed to Kill* (1980). "My fear," said Michael, "was that I would enjoy the part too much."

DUSTIN HOFFMAN
He played a woman so convincingly in *Tootsie* (1982) that one joker said that he should have been nominated for a Best Actress award.

CARY GRANT
Once admitted to having worn women's nylon panties—because they were easier to wash and pack. Dressed up as a woman in *I Was a Male War Bride* (1949).

DEBRA WINGER
Played a male angel in *Made in Heaven* (1987).

JACK LEMMON
Cross-dressed in *Some Like It Hot* (1959) with Tony Curtis. The coach hired to help him to walk like a woman gave up in dismay.
"I didn't want to walk like a woman," he said afterward, "I wanted to walk like a man trying to walk like a woman."

40 OTHERS WHO FOLLOWED SUIT (OR DRESS)

Tim Curry (*The Rocky Horror Picture Show*, 1975)
Linda Hunt (*The Year of Living Dangerously*, 1983)
Julie Andrews (*Victor/Victoria*, 1982)
Ed Wood, Jr. (*Glen or Glenda?*, 1952)

Rod Steiger (*No Way to Treat a Lady*, 1968)

John Lithgow (*The World According to Garp*, 1982)

Ethel Merman (*Airplane*, 1980)

Anne Heywood (*I Want What I Want*, 1972)

Johnny Depp (*Ed Wood*, 1994)

Theresa Russell (*Aria*, 1988)

Jaye Davidson (*The Crying Game*, 1992)

Harvey Fierstein (*Torch Song Trilogy*, 1988)

Patrick Swayze (*To Wong Foo, Thanks for Everything*, 1995)

Robbie Coltrane (*Nuns on the Run*, 1990)

Gene Hackman (*The Birdcage*, 1996)

Raquel Welch (*Myra Breckinridge*, 1970)

Dudley Moore (*Bedazzled*, 1967)

Bob Hope (*The Princess and the Pirate*, 1944)

Alec Guinness (*Kind Hearts and Coronets*, 1949)

George Sanders (*The Kremlin Letter*, 1970)

Greta Garbo (*Queen Christina*, 1933)

Marlene Dietrich (*Morocco*, 1930)

Nita Talbot (*A Very Special Favor*, 1965)

Signe Hasso (*The House on 92nd Street*, 1945)

Katharine Hepburn (*Sylvia Scarlett*, 1935)

Dick Shawn (*What Did You Do in the War, Daddy?*, 1966)

Bob Hope (*Casanova's Big Night*, 1954)

Bing Crosby (*High Time*, 1960)

Stan Laurel (*Jitterbugs*, 1943)

Lon Chaney (*The Unholy Three*, 1925)

Lionel Barrymore (*The Devil-Doll*, 1936)

William Powell (*Love Crazy*, 1941)

Alec Guinness (*The Comedians*, 1967)

Peter Sellers (*The Mouse that Roared*, 1959)

William Bendix (*Abroad with Two Yanks*, 1944)

Jimmy Durante (*You're in the Army Now*, 1951)

Lee J. Cobb (*In Like Flint*, 1967)
Ray Walston (*Caprice*, 1967)
Jerry Lewis (*Three on a Couch*, 1966)
Karen Black (*Come Back to the Five and Dime, Jimmy Dean, Jimmy Dean*, 1982)

YOU'RE NOT MY TYPE
15 stars on being typecast

BERT LAHR
"After *The Wizard of Oz* I was typecast as a lion, and there aren't all that many parts for lions."

ANDY GARCIA
"Typecast? I certainly hope so. I spent seven years without working and I have kids to bring up."

TROY DONAHUE
"After all those years playing Mr. Clean, I was afraid to comb my hair for fear of scratching my halo."

MURRAY F. ABRAHAM
"You keep getting the same role you got the Oscar for. Every time you complain, they don't change the script. They just offer you more money."

ESTHER WILLIAMS
"All they did at MGM was change my leading men and the water in my swimming pool."

JANET LEIGH
"I made musicals, comedies, and adventure films, but wherever I go, people only want to ask me about the shower scene in *Psycho*."

ALFRED HITCHCOCK
"If I made *Cinderella*, the audience would be looking for a body in the coach."

CHARLES BRONSON
"Some day I'd like a part where I can lean my elbow against a mantelpiece and have a cocktail."

EDWARD G. ROBINSON
"I was shot to death in six films between 1931 and 1937."

MICKEY ROONEY
"I was a 16-year-old boy for thirty years."

GLENN FORD
"I've never played anyone but myself on screen. No, I take that back. Once I tried to throw myself into the role of a Spanish gypsy. The picture was *The Loves of Carmen* with Rita Hayworth and it was the biggest bomb in history."

BORIS KARLOFF
"When I was 9 I played the demon king in *Cinderella* and it launched me on a long and happy life of being a monster."

SHIRLEY MACLAINE
"I've played so many hookers, film studios don't pay me in the usual way anymore; they just leave the money on the dressing table."

TONY CURTIS
"I was cast appropriately as a swindler in McCoy. Anyone who survives twenty-three years in Hollywood must be a con man."

JACK NICHOLSON
"When I got the part of the Devil in *The Witches of Eastwick*, many of my friends told me it was a classic example of type-casting."

FANGS AREN'T WHAT THEY USED TO BE

15 movie vampires

MAX SCHRECK, *Nosferatu* (1922)
The classic first screen incarnation of the Count.

DAVID NIVEN, *Vampira* (1974)
A suave Count Dracula abroad in Swinging London.

INGRID PITT, *The Vampire Lovers* (1970)
Everyone's favorite lesbian vamp.

GRACE JONES, *Vamp* (1986)
Grace feeds on "frat" boys in her seedy nightclub lair.

EDDIE MURPHY, *Vampire in Brooklyn* (1995)
Debonair black Nosferatu in the Big Apple.

KLAUS KINSKI, *Nosferatu the Vampyre* (1979)
Kinski gets his teeth into Isabelle Adjani.

GARY OLDMAN, *Dracula* (1992)
A sympathetic portrayal of the Count.

BELA LUGOSI, *Dracula* (1931)
"Listen, the children of the night."

CHRISTOPHER LEE, *Horror of Dracula* (1958)
Turned the Count into a charming and sexy aristocrat.

JACK PALANCE, *Dracula* (1973)
A dreadful piece of miscasting.

LESLIE NIELSEN, *Dracula: Dead and Loving It* (1995)
Mel Brooks and company give it the *Naked Gun* treatment.

LON CHANEY, JR. *Son of Dracula* (1943)
Swaps his wolf's clothing for a cape and fangs in the American
Deep South.

WILLIAM MARSHALL, *Blacula* (1972)
The Count gets the blaxploitation treatment.

GEORGE HAMILTON, *Love at First Bite* (1979)
Camp spoof set in N.Y.C.

TOM CRUISE, *Interview with the Vampire* (1994)
Plays Anne Rice's bored vampire Lestat.

NEVER SAY DIE
10 veterans who just wouldn't quit

JEANNE LOUISE CALMENT
114 years old when she appeared in *Vincent and Me* (1990).

WILLIAM H. TAYLOR
101 when he appeared in *Evangeline* (1929).

WALTER FIELD
Also 101 in *She's Too Hot to Handle* (1976).

ESTELLE WINWOOD
A ripe 93 in *Murder By Death* (1976).

LYDIA YEAMANS
Was 84 when she made her screen debut in *All Night* (1918), and
made over fifty films before she died eleven years later.

LILLIAN GISH
She was 93 when she appeared opposite Bette Davis in *The
Whales of August* (1986). Davis herself was no spring chicken at

78, making their collective ages an impressive 171.

CHARLES VANEL
This French actor was 95 when he made *Les Saisons des Plaisir* (1988), costarring opposite Denise Grey, a mere baby at 90.

GEORGE BURNS
Won an Oscar for *The Sunshine Boys* (1975) at the age of 80.

JESSICA TANDY
Tandy was also an octogenarian when she won the Best Actress Oscar for *Driving Miss Daisy* (1989).

MAURICE CHEVALIER
Was 79 when he made *Monkeys, Go Home* (1967).

BADFELLAS
10 unlikely screen villains

FRED MACMURRAY
Took the part of the murderer in *Double Indemnity* (1944) even after being told that it would destroy his reputation. Most other stars snubbed it.

ANTHONY HOPKINS
Took the part of Hannibal the Cannibal in *The Silence of the Lambs* (1991) even though it was considered tasteless. Went on to win an Oscar, become rich and famous, and create a cult movie.

TONY CURTIS
Hollywood's especial boy next door explored the dark side of his nature in *The Boston Strangler* (1968). "There's a bit of the

Boston Strangler in all of us," he said afterward, a comment that allegedly made Janet Leigh a little nervous.

SEAN CONNERY
Played the weather-changing Mr. Bad in *The Avengers* (1998)—an excruciatingly poor piece of hokum that he rightly disowned soon afterward.

GREGORY PECK
His "Angel of Death" performance as Joseph Mengele in *The Boys from Brazil* (1978) remains one of the bravest career changes in his entire *oeuvre* of decent souls rescuing damsels in distress.

OLIVER HARDY
Played screen villains before he teamed up with Stan Laurel for all those comedies.

RONALD REAGAN
A rare bad guy in *The Killers* (1964).

RICHARD WIDMARK
Began his career playing the giggling killer Tommy Udo in *Kiss Of Death* (1947). His star turn was a scene where he murders an old lady by kicking her wheelchair down the stairs.

ALAN ALDA
Goes ape in *Whispers in the Dark* (1992) as a freaky shrink who looks the picture of decency and good sense...until the final reel.

GEORGE CLOONEY
Clean-cut Dr. Ross plays a sick and ruthless killer alongside Quentin Tarantino in Robert Rodriguez's gun-crazy *From Dusk Till Dawn* (1995).

MAD, BAD, AND DANGEROUS TO WATCH

10 seminal moments of movie violence

Bonnie and Clyde (1967)
Beatty and Dunaway are spirited to a premature Boot Hill in slow motion after falling victim to the kind of firepower that might be used to quell a small South American *coup d'état*.

Psycho (1960)
Anthony Perkins (dressed as Mom) stands fuzzily poised outside a shower curtain with dagger raised in the air as he gets ready to slash the naked body of Janet Leigh to ribbons in a pioneering scattershot editorial montage by The Master.

Raging Bull (1980)
Robert de Niro breaking down in tears and primal screams as he bangs his head, fists, and elbows (in approximately that order) off a stone wall after being locked up for statutory rape.

Jaws (1975)
The ominous silence preceding the susurration of John Williams' score in the blue dawn light as a pretty girl has her leg champed off by a shark…and then silence again. Very subdued opening of a movie that is all too often accused of sensationalism.

The Shining (1979)
Jack Nicholson takes time off from his latest novel to greet wife Shelley Duvall with hatchet, gleaming dentures, and an original mating call: "Heeeeeeere's Johnny!"

Scarface (1983)
Al Pacino has already had enough bullets pumped into him to kill King Kong, but he still stands at the top of the *Gone with the Wind*-style staircase of his mansion with grenade launcher at the ready, telling all those hoods to give him their best shot (literally).

Apocalypse Now (1979)
The enormous, follicle-challenged Marlon Brando is carved up in a scene juxtaposed with the slaughter of an ox (you don't have to be Einstein to see the connection) in a familiar Francis Ford Coppola pastiche.

The Deer Hunter (1978)
The dementia of Christopher Walken as he plays Russian roulette: first because he has to, and then because he wants to. *The Dead Zone* previsited.

Reservoir Dogs (1992)
Michael Madsen performs an enthusiastic earectomy (sans anesthetic) on a cop he's tied to a chair, while grooving to the beat.

Taxi Driver (1976)
Robert de Niro, who looks as if butter wouldn't melt in his mouth, becomes a one-man army as he tries to get rid of the dirt at the core of the Big Apple.

TRUE CRIME
10 instances of real-life violence

CLINT EASTWOOD
Once fired a shot over a fan's head when she refused to leave a film set where he was working.

ROMAN POLANSKI
Threw a TV set through a window during the shooting of *Chinatown* (1974) when Jack Nicholson sccmcd more interested in watching a basketball game than in doing the next take.

ANTHONY QUINN
Nearly strangled his wife after waking up from a dream in which she featured as a panther about to devour him.

KIRK DOUGLAS
His father threw him through a door as a boy when he flicked a teaspoon at him.

ERROL FLYNN
Once glued a dog's eyelids together, and on another occasion he clipped a parrot's wings and made it dance on a hot metal tub. (He also liked putting snails on lime and watching them explode.)

SOPHIA LOREN
A fugitive from an asylum once attacked her with an ax, claiming that she was his lover.

JOAN CRAWFORD
Brutalized hcr four children for minor misdemeanors, as vividly chronicled in the Faye Dunaway biopic based on the book, *Mommie Dearest* (1981).

FRANK SINATRA

After George C. Scott beat Ava Gardner up, her former husband (one Francis Albert Sinatra) sent bodyguards to Scott's hotel room to rip the sleeves off a number of his coats. The message was clear: next time it would be his arms.

TONY CURTIS

His mother beat him senseless when he was young, apparently because she was jealous of his good looks.

LANA TURNER

Her father was murdered. Her daughter Cheryl stabbed her boyfriend Johnny Stompanato to death when he threatened to stab her.

W

THE BATTLE OF THE BULGE
5 dramatic weight changes for roles

ROBERT DE NIRO
Put on sixty pounds to play the part of Jake La Motta in *Raging Bull* (1980).

GARY OLDMAN
Lost so much weight to play Sid Vicious in *Sid and Nancy* (1986) that he had to be admitted to a hospital for malnutrition.

JENNIFER JASON LEIGH
Slimmed down to eighty-six pounds for the role of an anorexic in the TV movie *The Best Little Girl in the World* (1981).

JOHN GOODMAN
Says the day he realized that he had a weight problem was when he was told to lose a few pounds to play Babe Ruth in *The Babe* (1992).

RENEE ZELLWEGER
Put on 3 stone for *Bridget Jones' Diary* (2001).

HOW THE WEST WAS WON
10 westerns nominated for best picture at the Oscars

In Old Arizona (1928)
Cimarron (1930)
Stagecoach (1939)
The Ox-Bow Incident (1943)

High Noon (1952)
Shane (1953)
The Alamo (1960)
How the West Was Won (1963)
Butch Cassidy and the Sundance Kid (1969)
Dances with Wolves (1990)

(Only *Cimarron* and *Dances with Wolves* actually won.)

EYES THAT MEN ADORE AND A TORSO EVEN MORE SO
10 comments on women from Groucho Marx

"Anyone who says he can see through women is missing a lot."

"That's what I always say: love flies out the door when money comes innuendo."

"A man is only as old as the woman he's feeling."

"Young lady, I think you're a case of arrested development. With your development, somebody's bound to get arrested."

"I knew Doris Day before she was a virgin."

"Many years ago I chased a woman for almost two years, only to discover that her tastes were exactly like mine: we were both crazy about girls."

"Whoever named it necking was a poor judge of anatomy."

"Only one man in a thousand is a leader of men. The other 999 follow women."

"Mistresses are more common in California—in fact some of them are very common. It's easier for a man to conceal his mistress there because of the smog."

"Behind every screenwriter stands a woman—and behind her stands his wife."

AUTHOR! AUTHOR!
15 writers who appeared in films

Harold Pinter (*The Servant*, 1963)
Salman Rushdie (*Bridget Jones' Diary*, 2001)
Christopher Isherwood (*Rich and Famous*, 1981)
Martin Amis (*A High Wind in Jamaica*, 1965)
Peter Benchley (*Jaws*, 1975)
Allen Ginsberg (*Ciao Manhattan*, 1972)
Graham Greene (*Day for Night*, 1973)
Melvin Bragg (*The Tall Guy*, 1990)
Germaine Greer (*Universal Soldier*, 1992)
Stephen King (*Creepshow*, 1982)
Saul Bellow (*Zelig*, 1983)
Irvine Welsh (*The Acid House*, 1998)
James Dickey (*Deliverance*, 1972)
Quentin Crisp (*Orlando*, 1992)
Gore Vidal (*Gattaca*, 1997)

WAY BACK WHEN
10 stars in their youth

JIM CARREY

"I spent an awful lot of time in front of a mirror," he says, "staring at myself, watching how my face could change from laughter to tears. I spent my childhood pulling funny faces at myself, My mother always used to say that one day it would get stuck in some ridiculous expression and everybody would think I was the devil or crazy or from outer space."

DUSTIN HOFFMAN

His first memory is of having his hands tied to the side of his crib as a baby so that he couldn't bite his nails. (It didn't work, and he still does it.)

ELVIS PRESLEY

Had a twin brother Jesse, who died at birth. (Was this why Elvis felt he had to do twice as much as anyone else in life?)

SYLVESTER STALLONE

One of his childhood habits was "bizarrely" urinating into electrical sockets. (He also liked jumping off roofs with an umbrella in an attempt to be Superman.)

MADONNA

Her mother didn't allow her to use tampons because she felt that they were like having sex.

ANTHONY QUINN

When he was 3, his father told him that he had been born in a pigpen and adopted.

ROBIN WILLIAMS

He says his parents were always working, "so I was basically raised by the maid."

DREW BARRYMORE

Tried to kill herself at the age of 13 because of cocaine and alcohol addiction, and her inability to deal with the fame that came her way after she appeared in *E.T.*

LAURA DERN

Says she first became aware that her father (Bruce) was an actor when, at the age of 5, she watched *Hush Hush, Sweet Charlotte* on TV and saw Bette Davis fling his decapitated head down the stairs.

LANA TURNER

When she was 3, her mother took her to a train station. A woman appeared at the window of a passing train and Turner's mother said, "That's your real mother, not me." She had no reason for doing this besides playing a prank, but it traumatized Lana for years afterward.

Z

SEVERAL NIGHTS OF THE LIVING DEAD
10 incredibly strange zombie films

I Walked with a Zombie (1943)

Zombies on Broadway (1945)

Zombies of the Stratosphere (1952)

Zombies of Mora Tau (1957)

Incredibly Strange Creatures Who Stopped Living and Became Mixed-Up Zombies

(a.k.a. *The Teenage Psycho Meets Bloody Mary*) (1963)

Zombies of Sugar Hill (1974)

Dawn of the Dead (1978)

I Was a Zombie for the FBI (1982)

Zombie High (1987)

Pistol Whippin' Zombies (1998)

INDEX

INDEX

INDEX

INDEX

INDEX